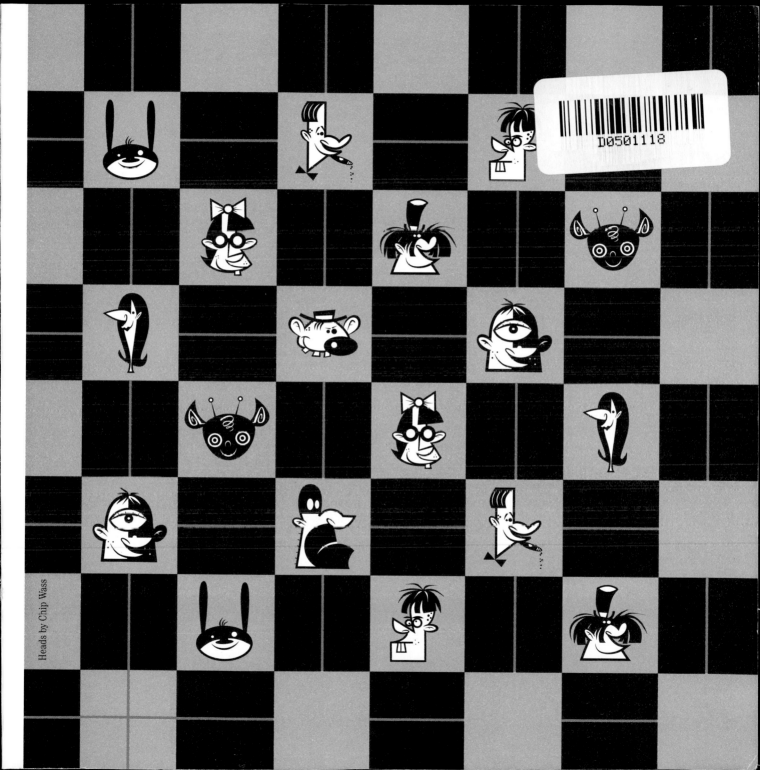

Heads by Chip Wass

THIS BOOK BELONGS TO:

The Happy Mutant Handbook

EDITORS
Mark Frauenfelder
Carla Sinclair
Gareth Branwyn

ONLINE DIRECTOR
Will Kreth

ART DIRECTOR
Georgia Rucker

RIVERHEAD BOOKS, NEW YORK

Riverhead Books
Published by The Berkley Publishing Group
200 Madison Avenue
New York, New York 10016

Copyright © 1995 by Mark Frauenfelder, Carla Sinclair, Gareth Branwyn, and Will Kreth.
Book design by Georgia Rucker
Cover illustration by Chip Wass

First edition: November 1995

Library of Congress Cataloging-in-Publication Data

The happy mutant handbook / [edited by] Mark Frauenfelder…[et al.].—1st ed.
    p. cm.
    ISBN 1-57322-502-9 (alk. paper)
    1. Subculture—United States. 2. Popular Culture—United States.
3. Social psychology—United States. I. Frauenfelder, Mark.
HN17.5.H345 1995
306'.1—dc20   95-9079
                                                CIP

Printed in the United States of America

10 9 8 7 6 5 4 3 2 1

CONTENTS

Chapter 3: Better Living Through Silicon

Chapter 4: Supreme Weirdos

Chapter 5: Toys and Cool Tools

Chapter 6: Brain Candy

FOREWORD

There's a weird intellectual pleasure in exploring the odd, the offbeat, and the arcane. It reminds me of when I was doing historical research for the novel *The Difference Engine*, set in the nineteenth century. You start the process by paging through the Official History. Then you dig back farther into the stuff that the official history mandarins merely footnote. There you find a reference to something that almost no authority is willing to cite. Then dig down just one more layer and: Whoa!

You stumble across some piece of scarcely documented ephemera that suddenly reveals, *hey* there was an *entire unsuspected other world* going on back there! Good Lord, I never realized that gay Catholic psychics from New Jersey levitated tables and blew spirit trumpets at the court of the Emperor Napoleon! Look, it's a book of London street slang all about counterfeiting and hookers! Christ, get a load of this leather case full of scary pig-iron *dental instruments*!

Suddenly you realize that deep beneath the shallow pretense of consensus reality was a whole parallel ecosystem . . . a pulsing culture like some kind of sulfur-gargling abyssal sealife. Ancient. Unsuspected. Primal. Chemosynthetic. Never saw daylight, never saw the sun. Wasn't *interested* in your sun. Had its *own* sun. Didn't *need* your sun. Getting along just fine down here by the hot fizzing volcanic fissure.

You can get just that exact kind of pleasurable alien shock from *The Happy Mutant Handbook*, only the real payoff is that this isn't some eldritch historical oddity, this is going on right now in our own society! It's not something exotically faraway and long-buried, it's nearby and walking around loose! It's happening here and now at the tag end of the twentieth century, and the authors and other culturati types are all still alive and mentally functional, pretty much, kind of!

This is a zine book, a true creature of the underground. Nobody ever stamped an official Seal of Cultural Approval on this baby. It arose because a couple of gifted slackers sprawling around on beanbags thought that starting their own magazine might, conceivably, be a nice way to kill time. No backers. No distributors. No big-name contributors. No venture capital, no brain trust. No audience. No market research. No demographic segmentation. Nothing but imagination and attitude. And now, five years later, this terrific book.

I dote on zines. I used to do a zine myself. I still write for zines. There are times when I really believe that zines and zine publishing are the most important things in the world. And this book is an emanation of the World's Greatest Neurozine. It's all thanks to Mark, Carla, and Gareth.

Mark and Carla are the gems of zinedom, zinedom's unlikely angels: some bent engineer from Colorado and his journalist manqué main squeeze. Why these two delightful people decided to publish their own private magazine, I never asked. Just one of those spontaneous sunny acts of theirs, apparently, like firing off (and igniting) a spraycan of Silly String. Gopod knows there's never been any money in the effort. And it's a lot harder work than their other favorite occupations, like staring raptly at grainy video of early '50s TV animation while munching outré plastic-wrapped Nipponese bonbons.

Carla and Mark, unlike many zine people, are not cranks or kooks. They appear to me to be the polar opposite of crankdom and kookdom: two of the very few primally sane people left in this sorry vale of tears. Granted, they may possibly be afflicted with some currently-undiagnosed futuristic turbo eight-legged postmodern groove-machine cranky kookdom, a very deep kooky crankdom that will only be deciphered centuries later through some kind of dense Toynbeean historical perspective and McLuhanesque media analysis. But that's somebody else's problem.

Like a lot of guys in my line of work, I subscribe to about 50 magazines. I'll buy dozens of other periodicals on a whim. However, *bOING bOING*, Mark and Carla's magazine, is without question my favorite magazine in the entire world. If *bOING bOING* and the sacred, much-admired *The New Yorker* were at the end of a pier together about to be tossed into murky seawater boiling with sharks, I would definitely save *The New Yorker*—because *bOING bOING* can walk on water and eats shark three times a week! *The New Yorker* is just some lousy goddamn magazine! bOING bOING is a cosmic emanation of interstellar ectoplasm.

It never fails to amaze me. *bOING bOING* is ruthlessly cheerful in its slaphappy study of postmodern life—often, some quite wicked and dreadfully depressing topics—and yet it never succumbs to any kind of deliberately upful pious bullshit. You'll never hear a single bogus whine about "unity" or "New Age" or "positivity" out of Mark and Carla's circle. What you will hear is jaded guffaws of antic laughter as Neo-Wobbly conspirators compare the finer details of Jack Chick tracts, duct tape, and pranks that scramble the frontal lobes of hapless normals. You'll find big shiny chunks of the full awful truth in their magazine and in this book, and also the ringing bell-like music of really cool people laughing heartily at the full awful truth. This book offers a unique and highly personal melange of well-forged irony and profoundly healthy cynicism. Stuff like this reaffirms your faith in the future and the human race.

Okay, well, this book doesn't exactly do all of that. It's just a book. I was just getting carried away. We live in a real world after all, and ought to pay more somber attention to our troubles and our moral defects. Let's face it, all the cool zines and with-it handbooks in the world won't help us if, for instance, the dreaded Greenhouse Effect really kicks in and the seas start rising and big sections of the world go underwater. However, thanks to *bOING bOING* and *The Happy Mutant Handbook*, I am now fully convinced of one thing. Even while we're all heaving sandbags at the angry rising foam, somebody out there will be scribbling Kilroys and happy faces on those sandbags with a Marks-a-Lot.

There are mutants thick as fleas now. Mutants are common as dirt. People are publicly claiming possession of American normality and the Western Canon who are basically humorless brownshirt psychopaths. Other wretched people claim an iron hammerlock on sensitivity and justice when they are really censorious Bolshevik social engineers. And then there are the wondrous, life-affirming, posthuman beings who wrote *The Happy Mutant Handbook*. They deserve your attention. They can really help you. They can change your life. And they won't ask you for money (at least, not for very much). These folks have been mutating simian brains since 1988. This is a crew of hardened technocultural veterans. This book offers to an unwitting global public an *umwelt* that has been tested by fire. This isn't so much a mere handbook as an entire means of perception. This is a rugged road-tested weltanschauung, ladies and gentlemen. And if you can stop giggling long enough, you'll find that these are mutants you can trust.

—Bruce Sterling

What Is a Happy Mutant?

Dear *Happy Mutant Handbook* Owner,

Congratulations on your purchase of *The Happy Mutant Handbook*! We're certain it will provide you with years of service.

What kind of service? you ask. Well, if you're like us, you are addicted to novelty. You're in constant need of brain candy, such as new ideas, entertainment, toys, and high weirdness. But it's hard to get your daily fix of neuro-stimulation by shopping for ready-made stuff, isn't it? Most mass-produced products, events, entertainment, and media have been designed to appeal to dimwits and "nervous nellie" types who would freak out if they ever suddenly found themselves a few inches away from the rest of the herd.

Face it, there's just not enough *ready-made* novelty to go around! To keep your brain from drying up and rattling around in your skull like a BB in an empty Silly Putty egg, you've got to constantly manufacture your *own* novelty. For instance, we, your editors, produce our own publication called *bOING bOING*. This allows us to meet interesting people and get lots of cool free stuff in the mail. We've also created our own Website so we can have fun with computer junkies on the Internet. Our purpose in writing this book is to let you in on the special formula so that you, too, can build your own perpetual novelty engines. Once you find out how much fun they are to make, you'll never put up with any of that store-bought false novelty again.

Still, some of you may be resistant to the idea of a do-it-yourself life. You say it's too expensive to buy the tools you need? That's a rotten excuse—in many cases the only tool you'll need is your brain, and in the long run, any tool you buy will pay for itself if you learn how to use it. And complaining that you don't have the "power" to change anything is an even more rotten excuse, especially after you learn how to redirect the energy of the mainstream "business-as-usual" world into creating a planet-sized theme park, with you playing the role of Supreme Commander!

By now, you're probably getting antsy and want to jump right in and begin using your nifty new handbook, but before starting, you have to promise to read the following stuff our lawyers made us include. You see, a lot of people think they are ready for novelty, but they aren't. Reading this book and acting on the information contained in it is going to reconfigure your nervous system. Not everybody wants this to happen to them, namely the two herds of earthlings called the Normals and the Unhappy Mutants.

So please examine the following information, which describes the characteristics of the three herds of humans that populate our planet. This will help you to determine whether or not this book is appropriate for you. If you fall into either the "Normal" or "Unhappy Mutant" category, you may wish to (1) stop reading this handbook immediately, and (2) refrain from acting on any of the information contained within. Failure to observe this warning may cause you to become very happy even if you wish to remain miserable. We will *not* be held responsible for anyone complaining that they were made happy against their will.

Chip Wass

THE THREE TYPES OF HUMAN BEINGS

NORMAL (*neophobe sixpackus*): Normals, who make up 90 percent of the human population, are people who avoid anything new, which they see as an unwelcome threat to their daily wage cycle. Their conformity-worshipping parents train them from birth to strive for predictability and "fitting in." Normals believe that predictability makes life safe and increases the chance of living long enough to breed and perpetuate their kind. Normals are very stable, and tend not to stray from their herd. Sometimes, however, when Normals undergo extreme shock, such as having a near-death or other "peak" experience, they begin to mutate. There are two basic types of Mutants, described below.

UNHAPPY MUTANT (*neophilic pessimisticus*): For whatever reason, Unhappy Mutants have dark and miserable attitudes. To escape their misery, they seek constant stimulation and new experiences. But they also like to do things that actually reinforce their lousy attitude (like watching the *Faces of Death* videos, and worshipping serial killers). They end up getting stuck in amplifying feedback cycles that lead to increasing misery and mopiness. When Unhappy Mutants crash and burn, they often "pole shift" and end up joining fundamentalist religions that enforce strict sets of beliefs and rules for living. These former Unhappy Mutants are called "Born-Again Normals," and behave like regular Normals on morality steroids.

HAPPY MUTANT (*neophilic optimisticus*) Like the Unhappy Mutant, Happy Mutants are also attracted to new ideas and activities. However, Happy Mutants do not seek novelty to escape misery. They seek it because they know that novelty opens up new possibilities for living a life filled with astonishment, wonder, and entertaining weirdness. Novelty is also highly addictive—the more you get, the more you want. It's important that Happy Mutants get frequent doses of novelty injected into their nervous systems, or they'll eventually revert to normality—a gruesome sight, indeed.

Have you decided which category you fit into? Not yet? To further illustrate the differences between the three types of humans, refer to the accompanying charts, HUMAN BEHAVIOR (fig. 1), and STUFF THAT THEY LIKE (fig. 2).

OK, now are you ready to start having fun? Great! Let's roll up our sleeves and get our tentacles dirty. There's a whole universe out there waiting to be tweaked! The following sections will introduce you to Reality Hacking (tweaking the mainstream for fun), Better Living Through Silicon (amplifying what you do through the use of computers and high-tech), Supreme Weirdos (who needs aliens and saucer people when we have a surplus of highly amusing kooks right here on Earth?), Toys & Cool Tools (to help you build and maintain those novelty engines), and Brain Candy (do-it-yourself media).

To get you in the right frame of mind, the next couple of pages outline a little of the Happy Mutant philosophy. Also, make sure to check out the six *neophilic optimistici* we proudly present in our Happy Mutant Hall of Fame. ◆

Note: If you want to share your ideas with us for future editions of the handbook, e-mail us at carla@well.com.

HAPPY MUTANT	NORMAL	UNHAPPY MUTANT
• Laughs at Authority • "Loves" kitsch culture • Uses computer tech for fun and empowerment • Do-it-yourself • Enjoys diversity, new ideas, complexity, "local color" • Thinks life is a gas • Looking forward to next cool book, tech, idea, Net site, goofy trend du jour	• Fears Authority • Loves kitsch culture • Works as keypunchin' meatbot for megacorporation • Buy it at K-Mart • Pines for "the good ol' days" • Has gas from overeating at Sizzler • Looking forward to early retirement	• Hates Authority • Loves death culture • Downloads "tasteless skin diseases" GIF files. • Steal it from friends • Thinks past, present, and future all suck equally • Likes to sniff all types of gas • Looking forward to dying in fiery crash or post office massacre

Fig. 2: *Stuff That They Like*

HAPPY MUTANT	NORMAL	UNHAPPY MUTANT
Brazil	*Sleepless in Seattle*	*Faces of Death*
bOING bOING	*People*	*ANSWER Me!*
They Might Be Giants	Janet Jackson	GG Allin
The Happy Mutant Handbook	*The Bridges of Madison County*	*Apocalypse Culture*
Silly Putty	Golf balls	Nunchakus
Basil Wolverton	Leroy Neiman	Joe Coleman
Church of the SubGenius	Church of Elvis	Church of Satan
Sea Monkeys	Irish Setter	Scorpion
Twister	Checkers	Russian Roulette
Archie McPhee	Lillian Vernon	Amok
"Why Be Normal?"	"I'm with Stupid"	"Charlie Don't Surf"
Pranks	White Collar Crime	Scams

THE MR. MAGOO THEORY

OF MUTANT PROGRESS

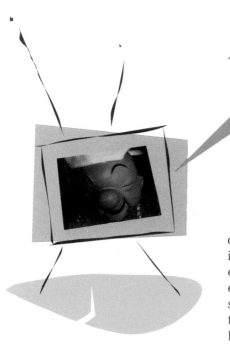

Gareth Branwyn

M r. Magoo's out for his morning stroll. Without knowing it, the nearsighted codger steps off the street into heavy traffic. The cars and trucks honk and swerve to miss him. They crash all around him in loud crunchy pileups. "Clumsy pedestrians!" barks Magoo. "By George, why don't people watch where they're going?"

Unbeknownst to the senile ol' bugger, he's headed straight for an open manhole. Just as he's about to step into the sewer opening, a hard hat pops up and Magoo steps on the worker's head, noticing nothing. In the course of his walk, dozens of other near disasters are averted by sheer

chance and serendipity. Magoo is ignorant all the while, usually blaming everyone around him for the negative events that he's triggered. He's testy, self-possessed, and his perceptions are totally warped, but strangely, he's happy . . . downright buoyant!

Anyone who's watched this goofy early '60s cartoon knows that Magoo's entire life is made up of these near mishaps. Mr. Magoo is not only oblivious to them, but almost always benefits from the chaos he creates: A prospector has spent his whole life looking for gold. Mr. Magoo stumbles on the motherlode and drives off with his car full of booty, completely clueless as to what's happened. The gold miner melts down in anger and despair as Magoo chaotically putt-putts home, negotiating dangerous mountain curves.

When you think about it, Mr. Magoo's exploits are a perfect metaphor for mutant progress. Like this hapless

cartoon geezer, we humans, in our nearsightedness, like to look down the path we've traveled and take credit for everything that's worked out, while conveniently ignoring (or blaming others for) all our screwups. In our arrogance, we can't see all the near disasters that chance has averted. Meanwhile, futurists try to develop forecasting methods to predict what's going to happen as we drive our fume-belching autos into the sunset— forget about it! Life's more chaotic, complex, and stranger than we could ever predict. It's far more realistic and fun to imagine the human experience as a Mr. Magoo episode where we're all merrily strolling through a low-budget cartoon backdrop, humming an ol' show tune, and playfully shaking our fists at all the morons who get in our way. As Magoo says: "Road Hog! Get outta my way!! By golly, whatever happened to gracious living?" ◆

Photo and illo by jorja

Ribofunk

Mark & Carla

Life Is the Ultimate Happy Mutant

Cyberpunk is a world of silicon chip implants, stainless steel, virtual reality, and grim computer hackers. It's fun to read about, but who wants to live that way? Happy Mutants would rather dance to the beat of Ribofunk, a designer-lifestyle term coined by science fiction author Paul DiFilippo, where the hot stickiness of "ribo" (as in ribonucleic acid) replaces the cold, mechanical control-circuit aspect of "cyber," and the sweaty, organic yowl of "funk" drowns out the angry no-future buzz of "punk." As author Kevin Kelly points out in his Cyberpunk-meets-Ribofunk book, *Out of Control*, technology and natural systems are now merging. The table here will give you an idea of what's in store. ◆

CYBERPUNK	Ribofunk
silicon	carbon
computer hacking	biohacking
designer drugs	designer genes
control	chaos
cyborg	mutant
implants	parasites
Neuromancer	*Blood Music*
logic	libido
Kraftwerk	George Clinton
robotics	artificial life
Chess	Twister

Cicciolina:

The Little Fleshy One

Gareth Branwyn

Cicciolina is the world's embassadress of love. A porn star, performance artist, politician, stuffed animal enthusiast, and snake charmer, she shocked and delighted the world in 1987 when she was elected to the Italian Parliament. Many people believed her nomination was originally an attempt at cynical commentary on the state of Italian politics, but it backfired when she was actually elected. The embarrassed Partito Radicale gently pressured her to forfeit her seat, but she refused. "I want to be the Minister of Culture," was her reply.

Born Ilona Staller in 1952, Cicciolina (which has been reported to mean "Little Cuddly," "Little Fleshy One," and "Little Cabbage") rose to fame in Italy as a hardcore porn actress. Like Betty Page, and a handful of other such stars, Cicciolina had an appearance of innocence and authenticity that made her different from her co-stars. She seemed to be floating through her films, on her own mission of love, even when things around her were totally depraved. Her films include *Backfield in Motion* and *The Rise of the Roman Empress* (*I & II*).

She served in the parliament from '87 to '92. During that time, Cicciolina managed to stay in the limelight through a number of outrageous acts and proclamations. Upon taking office, she offered to have sex with any other member who was in need. She offered herself to the Italian troops stationed in the Persian Gulf ("I want to bring a little bit of Christmas cheer and relief to those poor cuddlies . . . "), and even offered to screw Saddam Hussein, claiming it would bring peace to the Middle East. Cicciolina likes to dress like a little girl, wear crowns made out of flowers, and carry stuffed animals with her. She kisses and squeezes them whenever she gets overly excited.

Cicciolina has quit politics and now wants to take her "make love/not war" message to the masses via a daytime talk show. One can only imagine what she'd do on her own TV show. ◆

Eric White

Theodore Geisel:
Seuss I Am!

Mark Frauenfelder

One of my favorite stories is *The Sneetches* by Dr. Seuss. The Sneetches were a trendy, jealous species of animal that had established a pecking order based on the markings (or absence of markings) on their bellies. Sneetches with a star were considered cooler than the starless ones. Along came an opportunistic monkey with a mustache, Sylvester McMonkey McBean, who brought with him a couple of machines that could add or remove the stars. One second after selling the last starless Sneetch a trip through his "Star On Machine," McBean convinced the whole lot that the hip look was au naturel, so the Sneetches lined up in front of the "Star Off Machine." Pretty soon he had the Sneetches running from the exit of one machine directly to the entrance of another. There's a great two-page spread in the book that has the Sneetches in a long figure-eight line, waiting to go through the rubbery, wheezing star machines. The monkey stands in the middle of the chaos, collecting a huge pile of money from the panicked Sneetches.

Born Theodor Seuss Geisel in 1904, Dr. Seuss created far-out worlds full of wonderful machines and strange beasts that have fueled the minds of artists, scientists, and inventors-to-be since 1937.

After being rejected by 28 publishing houses in New York, Seuss met up with an old school chum who worked for a publishing company. His buddy could sense that Seuss was onto something and published *And to Think That I Saw It on Mulberry Street*.

His books were immensely popular, and he went on to publish forty-eight, including *Bartholomew and the Oobleck* (1949), *Horton Hears a Who* (1954), *The Cat in the Hat* (1957), *How the Grinch Stole Christmas* (1957), *Green Eggs and Ham* (1960), and *The Lorax* (1971).

The gentle doctor died in his sleep in 1991. No doubt he was dreaming of a Crayola-colored land filled with his fantastical friends. ◆

Eric White

Timothy Leary: Happy Mutant at Large

Mark Frauenfelder

HM Hall of Fame

On a beautiful summer day in Cuernavaca, Mexico, 1960, Dr. Timothy Leary, a 39-year-old professor of psychology at Harvard, stuffed a handful of psychedelic mushrooms into his mouth, and washed them down with beer. He had never even smoked pot before. By evening he was a changed man. "In the four hours by the swimming pool in Cuernavaca I learned more about the mind, the brain, and its structures than I did in the proceeding fifteen as a diligent psychologist," he wrote in his autobiography, *Flashbacks*. His trip into the inner recesses of his neocortex got Leary interested in psychedelic drugs as a tool to explore and program the human brain, which he considered an "underutilized biocomputer." He returned to Harvard and turned on over 300 people, including priests and prisoners, with then-legal psilocibin and LSD. Harvard officials considered his work irresponsible, however, and booted him from the university in 1963.

Eventually, Leary wound up in prison for possession of a single joint. Faced with a thirty-year sentence, he escaped from prison by going hand-over-hand across a 20-foot-high telephone wire.

He fled the country and went to Europe, and then Algiers, to stay with Black Panther Eldridge Cleaver. When things got weird between the professor and the Black Panther, Leary went to Afghanistan, where U.S. agents found him and hauled him back to Folsom high security prison in January 1973.

In prison, Leary wrote some of his most interesting and influential books, including *Exo-Psychology, The Intelligence Agents*, and *The Game of Life*. In September 1975, after being shuffled around various prisons (a total of 36 during his career), he was released.

In the following years, Leary became interested in life extension (he's arranged to have his head preserved in liquid nitrogen when he dies), space exploration, and most recently, computer technology, which he considers a useful tool for personal freedom and consciousness tweaking.

Through all his ordeals, Leary has remained bright, curious, and optimistic about life. His guiding principles remain "think for yourself" and "question authority," and his ultimate goal is to "take charge of evolution." ♦

Eric White

Sun Ra:
Saturnian Shaman
of Sound

Will Kreth

HM Hall

"*Some call me Mr. Ra, some call me Mr. Re, but you can call me Mr. Mystery.*" So said the late, enigmatic Sun Ra—jazz bandleader, arranger, keyboard player, and shaman of sound. Erroneously reported by the straight world as having been born on May 22, 1914, as Herman "Sonny" Blount in Birmingham, Alabama, Ra was actually born on Saturn "around 5,000 years ago—give or take a few minutes"—as he was quick to point out.

Touring the world starting in 1956, with his big band, the "Intergalactic Arkestra," Ra made a convincing case for his non-terrestrial origins. Adorned in outlandish costumes, with silver chain-mail skullcaps and long, flowing robes emblazoned with glittery splashes of gold and silver lamé, he captivated audiences from Paris to Tokyo to New Orleans. Ra recorded over 200 albums (on his own label), with titles like *Cosmic Tones for Mental Therapy*, *Sun Ra Visits Planet Earth*, and *The Heliocentric Worlds of Sun Ra*.

Unlike the stereotype of heroin-addled jazzbos, Ra did not tolerate drugs in his Arkestra. It was a Betty Ford Clinic kind of outfit. With masses of wailing brass polyphony over a bed of Afro-Latin percussion, Ra used call-and-response chants, dancers, and light shows. He was one of the first working musicians in the world to embrace the Moog synthesizer, which certainly upped the space music ante with its sci-fi sonority.

Financially, playing in Sun Ra's Arkestra was a disaster for its members —it's obvious that his players were doing it for the love of the music. Sun Ra's Arkestra stayed together through the anti-jazz era of the '70s and '80s. In recent years, he was enjoying a comeback and a new generation of fans—some, no doubt, the children of the parents who saw him in the 1960s.

He said: "All of nature's really music. Movement is mere rhythm, you see. The sun moves in rhythm; it's right on time . . . I get my authority from the ruler of the planet. I'm here to make it a better place . . . This planet has got to be tuned up to the right key, like they do with a piano. I've dedicated my life to rescuing the people of this planet."

Sun Ra blew this popsicle stand called Earth on May 30, 1993, but he is no doubt just off tuning up some other world. ◆

Eric White

Lady Lovelace:
The Enchantress of Numbers

Betty Toole

In 1976 I went to the Science Museum in London to see Charles Babbage's Analytical Engine, a proto-computer from the early 19th century. Next to it was a portrait of a very beautiful young woman. Her name was Ada Byron (also known as Lady Lovelace), and she turned out to be one of the most colorful characters in computer history.

Ada Byron's life, like her father's, Lord Byron, was short (36 years), and like her father, she has evoked images of "mad and bad and dangerous to know." William Gibson and Bruce Sterling used her as a character in their novel *The Difference Engine*. Her friends included Charles Babbage, Charles Dickens, and Michael Faraday, as well as some less savory characters. Her interests ranged from music to gambling to computers.

Ada wrote a 64-page article describing Charles Babbage's Analytical Engine (now regarded by many as the first computer) and not only conceived of computer programming, but predicted that computers might be used to compose complex music, to produce graphics, and be used for both practical and scientific use.

Her letters to Babbage, are as fascinating as her description of the first computer, and are laced with language (most likely due to her being on the opiate drug laudanum) that is both practical and poetical: "I am working very hard for you: like the Devil in fact: (which perhaps I am) . . . No one knows what almost awful energy & power lie yet undeveloped in that wiry little system of mine."

When done writing her article about the Analytical Engine, after some typical male-female arguments, she invited Babbage to her home in Somerset. Babbage accepted the invitation by writing: "Forget this world and all its troubles and if possible its multitudinous charlatans—everything in short but the Enchantress of Numbers." ◆

Eric White

William M. Gaines:

The Worry-Free

Madman

Carla Sinclair

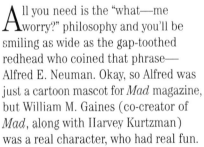

Eric White

All you need is the "what—me worry?" philosophy and you'll be smiling as wide as the gap-toothed redhead who coined that phrase— Alfred E. Neuman. Okay, so Alfred was just a cartoon mascot for *Mad* magazine, but William M. Gaines (co-creator of *Mad*, along with Harvey Kurtzman) was a real character, who had real fun.

The fun began at Educational Comics, owned by Bill's father, Max Gaines. Soon after Bill got a job at EC as a gofer, his dad died in a boating accident. Bill then took over the company, changed EC to Entertaining Comics, and revolutionized not only the world of comics, but American humor as well.

Beginning with *The Crypt of Terror* and *The Vault of Horror* in 1950, Gaines launched a new genre of comic books—horror and suspense. EC's grisly tales clutched the imaginations of American youth, and comic book sales boomed at an astounding rate. Unfortunately, the media was already worshipping a name-calling, finger-pointing morphine junkie by the name of Joe McCarthy, who flew into a fanatic rage over these grisly tales. Humans were squirming with devilish delight over these comics—they were having too much fun! Paranoia was *tres chic*, and by 1954 McCarthy's gang put an end to Gaines's line of horror comics.

Gaines had already launched *Mad* magazine, however, so he just shifted gears, and yet another genre was born —the American satire magazine. *Mad* poked fun at other comic books, and any 2- or 3-dimensional character who happened to be in the way. It was a tremendous success. Its dramatic impact on American humor influenced bigwigs such as *Saturday Night Live*, '60s cartoonist Robert Crumb, satirical films like *Airplane* and *Naked Gun*, and my own b*OING* b*OING* magazine.

Although he left this planet in 1992 after circling the sun 70 times, the Happy Mutants of the world will be here to perpetuate his "what—me worry?" attitude. ♦

Reality Hacking

R.U. Sirius

"I am made of media." —Mark Leyner

Reality hacking—designer lifestyles and pranks that playfully interrupt the scheduled programming of the masses—is a way of life for Happy Mutants. I prefer to believe that reality hacking began in 1987 when I invented the phrase to rename the psychedelic magazine *High Frontiers. Reality Hackers* was a magazine about the ways that our realities are being hacked by technology and media, as well as drugs. (The name was later mutated once again to *Mondo 2000*, after our distributor told us that stores didn't want to carry it because "people think it's a weird Charlie Manson cult magazine from California about hacking people up.")

On the other hand, reality hacking probably started with cave paintings, one of the earliest forms of media. Prehistoric graffiti artists discovered the power of symbols in shaping the viewer's perception of reality. The big shots of the cave clans used symbols not only to change the way their minions perceived the world around them, but also to convince them that *imaginary* things, like gods and demons, existed. This was very useful for keeping the grunt workers in line. So useful, in fact, that more sophisticated ways of symbol transmission were soon invented, such as smoke signals and satellite TV.

For thousands of years, only the people with lots of money could afford to transmit their version of reality. But in the last decade or so, media technology has become so cheap that almost anyone can buy a modem, publish a zine, or set up a pirate radio station and get in on the reality hacking business. Other pranksters have figured out ways to use the existing mass media machinery as an inexpensive vehicle to carry satirical messages to the masses.

The following section is about people who refuse to accept the role of an audience member in the media circus. They've figured out how to be part of the show. By learning the few simple tricks and ideas presented here, you can hack reality, too. ♦

Claudia Newell

Jerod Pore

Do-it-yourself

Radio & TV

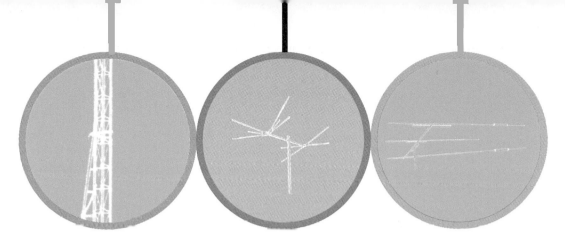

"We want the airwaves!"—The Ramones

It's fun sharing information. That's why people publish minicomics, form Internet mailing lists, and produce electronic zines. If there's a way to report something interesting, enterprising folks have figured out how to do it, and do it cheaply.

But one otherwise excellent medium is harder to crack than magazines or modems: radio. While almost every home in the United States is loaded with radios and TV receivers, very few homes contain radio or television transmitters. This is because the FCC, a government agency formed in 1934 to regulate the airwaves, began requiring that people have a license to broadcast radio signals. You can guess what happened. Mutants got the short end of the stick. To make matters worse, in 1987 the FCC decreed that a radio or TV station could lose its license if it broadcast anything considered by the FCC to be indecent. Whenever a government bureaucracy restricts the free flow of information, smart people

find a workaround, and set up another channel for the information to flow. The FCC's silly un-American rule was the best thing anyone could have done to promote do-it-yourself broadcasting.

Even though the goons of the FCC are out there, roaming the streets in unmarked vans, eager to break down doors, seize everything vaguely electronic, and slap home broadcasters with a $10,000 Notice of Apparent (!) Liability, the urge to liberate information is too strong to be squashed.

But before we start with the how-to stuff, here's the obligatory condom talk: While transmitting without a license is illegal, it's an even bigger offense to interfere with another transmission. Jamming Rush Limbaugh is a guaranteed ticket to jail (unless you build a disposable transmitter and leave it broadcasting from someplace you never plan on being near again).

Okay, enough legal junk, let's get started! First, do you want to broadcast TV, AM, FM, or shortwave signals? Shortwave has its romance; your

signal can bounce from Missoula to Kazakhstan, and it's filled with propaganda from enemy nations. You can simply purchase (as opposed to build from a kit) all the used equipment you need from your local ham radio club. But the shortwave spectrum is huge, so finding a shortwave pirate transmission is almost as much work as broadcasting one. Also, the transmission ranges depend on the weather. And while almost everyone has an FM radio, few people in the U.S. have shortwave receivers. (Yet the FCC is most vicious with shortwave pirates. Go figure.)

AM radio is tricky, and requires a large, noticeable antenna if you want to cover a fair distance. Plus AM is very susceptible to outside interference. While your potential audience is huge, the AM spectrum is already overflowing with broadcasters. (Remember that rule about jamming another broadcast! Very few pirates broadcast over AM and those that do don't do so for long.) Do-it-yourself AM is not recommended.

TV is even riskier, although technically easier than radio. How

easy? Plug an amplifier and antenna into the output jack of a VCR and you're on channel 3 in your immediate vicinity. While there are consumer products for broadcasting your VCR around your house, slight modifications can make them cover blocks. The most successful free TV projects are in rural areas.

The best way to go is FM. You can't buy an off-the-shelf FM transmitter in the United States, at least not one that will broadcast farther than you can spit. You can buy some easily assembled kits from Ramsey, Free Radio Berkeley, and Panaxis (see resource guide). Prices range from $30 to $300, depending on how much oomph you want. Everyone who uses a Panaxis raves about it. If you're in a rural area where a low-power FM transmission is unlikely to catch the attention of the FCC, you should consider buying a real transmitter from them. If you're in a denser area, where a smaller transmitter with a range of a few blocks can mean reaching hundreds or even thousands of listeners, you can go even cheaper. A few entrepreneurs are popping up, selling cheap transmitters that they have built themselves for about $25 (check out

alt.radio.pirate). The advantage of a $25 transmitter is that you can ditch it if the FCC is breathing down your antennae. Also, broadcasts can be prerecorded and a Walkman-style tape player can be attached to the transmitter. This way you can broadcast from a car or, better yet, an abandoned building or park with a couple of escape routes.

An FM transmitter can be built in half an hour with less than $15 in parts. I've seen people who can barely operate a soldering iron put together a transmitter from a shopping list of electronic parts.

The resources listed below are a great way to get started. Having your own radio station might not get people to take their clothes off for you (unless you also happen to be Christian Slater in the pirate radio romance *Pump Up the Volume*), but it's one heck of a great way to make some noise. Have fun, and don't get caught! ◆

RESOURCES

Ramsey Electronics: 793 Canning Parkway Victor, NY, 14564. 716/924-4560, fax 716/924-4555.

Panaxis Productions: PO Box 130, Paradise, CA, 95967-0130. 916/534-0417.

Mycal offers a guide to building transmitters. Mycal: PO Box 750381 Petaluma, CA 94975-0381. e-mail: mycal@netacsys.com.

On Usenet check out alt.radio.pirate, as well as the legitimate rec.radio groups.

Stephen Dunifer heads Free Radio Berkeley and sells the FRB kit (7 watts of output) for $55. e-mail: frbspd@crl.com.

There are ftp archives at dg-rtp.dg.com /fm10 (for Ramsey) and crl.com /users/ro/frbspd (for Free Radio Berkeley).

Shortwave pirate wannabes should get a copy of *The ACE* from PO Box 11201, Shawnee Mission, KS 66207-0201.

Invasion of the Paper Smiles

Imagine a smiley-face drawn on a paper plate with a thick black marker. Now imagine seeing hundreds of them plastered on street signs, telephone poles, bus benches, and other city fixtures. The strange smiles greet you every day for weeks, even months. When they are torn down by irritated city workers, they are replaced by fresh ones overnight. A year later you still spot these eerie happy faces staring down at you as you speed along the freeway. Anxiety sets in. Where are these generic smiles coming from? What do they mean? Who's messing with your mind???

The above scenario is something that's been going on in Los Angeles for years now. Many pranksters specialize in playing anonymous tricks on the masses. Instead of tweaking the minds of one or two humans, they'd rather play with a whole city full of people. They quietly infiltrate an urban area with familiar yet unsettling symbols or words, and then kick back and watch as the populace is swept into a cloud of confusion and paranoia.

We called the Cacophony Society and other prankmasters, but to no avail. Nobody seems to know where these devilish smiles are coming from. We are baffled.

While obsessing over the plates, we were surprised at the amount of fuzzy-headed people who denied ever seeing them. But we fixed that. We took these unaware folks on a smiley-face tour, and have been informed that these people haven't been able to put their blinders back on. They see the uncanny smiles everywhere now!

Last time I went to LA, I noticed that some of the plates have weathered and smeared from the rain, making them look more ominous and grotesque than ever before. Other plates, however, are fresh and crisp, reminding us edgy citizens that THEY are still out there. ◆

Carla Sinclair

MR. EVERYMUTANT SEZ ™

I SURVIVED THE **ONSLAUGHT** OF IMAGE SATURATION, **POST-HUMAN** COMMODIFICATION AND THE SUBARU LEGACY WITH THE HELP OF

(YOUR BRAND HERE)

Fig. 1

A Guide to Personal Brand Names

Brought to you by Beatnik World Servicing, A division of ASAP Systems and Shawn Wolfe Associates Inc.

AFTER ALL! WHAT WE'RE DEALING WITH HERE IS A COMBINED HORROR OF AND COMPELLING FASCINATION WITH *'THE MASS PRODUCED'*, WITH YOU KNOW, *'CULTURAL HOMOGENIZATION'*!

Fig. 2

Face it, even the happiest mutants often feel defined not so much by what they think or do, but rather by what brand of product they choose to buy. At one time, brands were used to identify products, but now it's the consumers who are branded as labels, which have moved from the inside of garments to the outside and all over the person, literally from head to toe.

Trying to "kick" the brand name habit won't help. It only leads to another line of "clear," "lite," or "simple" products, new consumer frontiers for the herd to orbit.

No, the answer isn't avoiding brand names, it's developing your own "personal brand name." Instead of struggling to keep your nose above water in a polluted sea of advertising messages, a personal brand can lift you out of the submissive dog-paddling position that devolved, bottom-feeding end users assume (see fig. 1).

The personal brand steals the power of the corporate name brands, which "take over" as mute puppet dictators of the soul. And since the power is always in the brand, never in what the brand represents, your personal brand needs no product to back it up (see fig. 2). It's an advertisement for its own present and future uselessness, a mocking symbol of all that is bought and sold,

Fig. 3

The personal brand that will serve as a shield against these forces might also, ideally, be used to act ON them. Picture, if you must, actual shields, one for each hand. One is marked "2+2=4." The other is marked "2+2=5." Both are useful to the Wee Brand Warrior: Wielder Of The Personal Brand. (It will be necessary for you to master and make use of such ill-logic if you are to successfully fight these fires with your own.)

Fig. 4

The twisted psychology of the corporate logo now made simple! (And you can bet there is by now a psychologist somewhere using Burger King and Pepsi and AT&T logo flashcards as therapeutic aids.)

but this time for its very own sake and for yours. The logic of personal branding is the knowledge that turns Joe Camel slowly and painfully inside out forever and ever (see fig. 3).

Your personal brand will act as a sort of antibody in the system of symbols and messages that we all move in. Heroically, you will swim into the brainwashing Niagara of logos, ads, and lifestyle imagery that crashes down on you. Your personal brand will be designed to serve as a shield against such toxic showers.

The practical applications of a personal brand are dubious, and rightly so. "Practical" has become a tired selling word in the so-called "New Age" and cannot be trusted. The practice of personal branding can, however, be a sheer, perverse, and necessary joy. The alternative to this sort of activity is to take it lying down: the famed path of least resistance. And this, of course, is exactly what "they" want you to do.

An important part of any anti-marketing strategy is a trademark or logo. The logo itself will often carry the full weight and effect of your personal campaign. No personal brand is complete without one. And you need no design experience or special facilities to devise one! You don't necessarily

Fig. 5

Sloganeering in action: "Visualize a world that is an orbiting advertisement for its own ultimate uselessness." "I brake for advertising." "Consumer Parasite Onboard." Remember, Andre Breton said the world would end, not with a good book, but with a beautiful advertisement for heaven or for hell.

Fig. 6

need a "name," even. An inkblot with a little TM in the corner could be sufficient for your purposes (see fig. 4). In fact, you can dispense with the inkblot if you like, and just use the TM by itself as the distilled, mineral essence of trademarking and corporate paranoia itself.

When applying your logo, be endlessly repetitious and "tag" often, wherever you go. Whether driving home the same (non)message over and over again or just leaving your mark, the numbing effects that the big brands enjoy are achieved with blind repetition through broadcast and mass production. A reproducible, stick-on logo makes this a snap. As you may know, logos have strange and hypnotic powers. Make friends with your logo and learn to harness its unique brand of power. As an experiment, photocopy your logo (10

or 20 on a sheet) and run off as many as you can afford. Spread hundreds of them out on the floor (enough to fill your cone of vision) and notice the sinister alien life they assume. Notice your logo's floating, familiar, and strangely unlocatable "presence."

If you aspire to concoct fake ads or real bumper stickers (see fig. 5) you will want to say more than who you are and that you were here. This is where an encapsulated thought, in the form of a "slogan" will be useful. When coming up with slogans, say whatever you wish, but be advised: It is important to make a mockery of

and to drain meaning from the language used by today's marketing geniuses. Utilize key buzzwords like Lifestyle, Alternative, New, Real, Improved, Recycled, Complete, System, Classic . . . Feel free to combine them all into a meaningless, clustered absurdity (see fig. 6).

The opportunities for brand proliferation and personalization are plentiful. You say you want a clear stick-on logo for the lower corner of your TV screen? You say you want to mint your own private form of currency? The facilities at any copy shop make possible the professional and seamless fabrication of everything from "fake" letterhead to phony laminated I.D. badges to annoying poster-size ads to full color T-shirts. Likewise, all forms of customized mugs, calendars, pencils, fobs, even wristwatches with "your logo here" are cheaply had. Every

Fig. 7

in-flight magazine is peppered with such offers for the "entrepreneur." (A logo wristwatch will run you about $20.)

You will find fake letterhead and business cards to be extremely useful in the acquisition of free and bizarre catalogs and trade publications you never knew existed. And trade publications each contain what is called a "bingo card." A "bingo card" is a little business reply card printed with hundreds of numbers that each correspond to a company that advertised in the magazine. Circle the numbers of the companies from which you'd like to receive "more information," send in the card, then sit back and watch your mailbox choke on more obscure junk mail than you've ever seen. As proprietor of a fake company, cool "samples" from all varieties of vendors, publishers, manufacturers, and public relations departments will be yours for the asking. (As anyone who has ever published a music fanzine knows: Even flimsy Xeroxed PR will produce a steady flow of "promotional" records and tapes from all over the world.) Also, the feigned authority of a convincing corporate letterhead can be used with abandon to register all forms of bizarre complaints and "leveraged warnings" to corporate thugs and elected officials!

Use your personal brand liberally. Have fun with it(see fig. 7). Leave your mark on this already hopelessly Xeroxed and marked up world of ours. Branding has been part of life since before the tree this book was printed on was even planted! Personal Branding, as a way of life, may just save your mutant soul. So don't be lost in the extinction shuffle! Be Happy! Mutate! Evolve! And above all ADVERTISE! ◆

Cold Shoulder

Carla Sinclair

One of the simplest forms of reality hacking is the good old-fashioned phone prank. Using the telephone can be a very cheap, convenient, and creative way to shake the torpor out of your average drone. And ideas for crank calling are endless! I had some fun with the Alcor Life Extension Foundation. This cryonics institution freezes human heads and bodies immediately after a person dies in hopes of reviving them at a later date. I couldn't resist! Read on . . .

A • (*receptionist*) Alcor Foundation.
C • Yes, hi, I'd like to speak to someone in the freezing department.
A • The what?!
C • You know, the people in charge of signing people up.

A • Uh, one moment please. Your name?
C • My name is Carla.
(*pause*)
A • Hi, this is Derek Ryan.
C • Hi! This is Carla. I live in Los Angeles, and I was wondering how much it would cost to freeze my arms.
A • To freeze your *arms*??
C • Yeah.
A • Hmm (*nervous chuckle*) uhh, actually, that's not something I think we've ever done. I don't know if it's something we would ever do. But I'd be the wrong person to talk to about that. I'm the membership administrator, I get people signed up for cryonics.
C • Well, what other parts have you

frozen then?
A • Well, we either freeze a person's whole body or just their head. Can you explain to me why it is you only want your arms frozen?
C • Because that's the best part of my body.
A • Er . . . um . . . a . . . (*another nervous chuckle*) Are you talking about after your death you want them frozen?
C • Well, yeah. Everyone *always* compliments my arms. My arms are great. So I want to freeze them.
A • Hmm, well, why don't you hold on a second.
C • Okay.
(*pause*)
A • Hi, it's Derek again. Uh, I just spoke with our vice president,

Danny Hellman

(A Good Ol' Fashioned Phone Prank!)

and he said that's just something we cannot do.

How come?

A • Well, he didn't give me specific reasons for it, but he was very emphatic.

C • What does *that* mean?

A • Well I, uh, he was, (*chuckle*) it's definitely, uh . . .

C • No?

A • Yeah, definitely (*chuckle*) that we, we, we won't do that. Our basic purpose is, uh, the uh . . .

C • Well, what if somebody needs arms later on? Mine would be great.

A • Well, actually, uh, I don't know how much you know about cryonics or anything, but uh, by the time we have the technology to bring these people out of suspension, the actual cloning of cells will be a very simple thing. You might want to have your tissue samples stored at a tissue storage bank or something. That's where

the pattern that makes your arms what they are is—in your DNA. But, uh, our basic purpose is people who want to take the chance to continue to live by having themselves frozen when and if they die. But we're not really here to freeze body parts.

C • Hmm, well you said that you just freeze heads.

A • Well, when we just freeze heads it still carries out our main motivation, which is getting the person to the future. Your brain is basically what contains who you are. You can cut off your hand or your arm, and you still have all your memories, all of your personality. Of course you'd still be psychologically altered, but you would be the same person. Whereas, if I cut off a part of your brain, uh, you would be a completely different person. The basic reasoning for just freezing your head is that the technology

required to reverse what's wrong with the patient, you know, what caused them to die in the first place will be much more advanced technology than that required to just clone cells . . .

C • Oh boy.

A • . . . and basically just grow a whole new body.

C • Huh. Well, I really wouldn't want to just leave my brain.

A • Well, if you don't freeze your brain, then you're not really freezing you, you're just freezing a part of you. Our interest isn't really in having organ donations or body-part donations—it's in attempting to transport people to the future, where technology can repair what's wrong with them and help them to continue their life.

C • Oh, I don't think my brain is smart enough for that.

A • Okay. No problem.

C • Well, thank you! ♦

PLAN AHEAD

SOMETHING

FISHY

ARTIFICIAL

ART OFFICIAL

Colin Berry

It was in 1986 that Los Angelenos first awoke to find an unflattering poster of Ronald Reagan and three cronies staring from hundreds of traffic-light switching boxes at intersections across the city. Bearing the slogan "Men With No Lips," the poster marked the first of a series of nonsanctioned portraitures that would, over the next decade, mysteriously appear in cities across the country, featuring the garishly painted and beguiling likenesses of George Bush, Dan Quayle, Jim and Tammy Faye Bakker, Jesse Helms, Daryl Gates, and a dozen other white-collar politicos and public figures. The portraits, painted and pasted by LA artist Robbie Conal, combined the saturation and consistency of an ad campaign with the outspokenness of a high-profile political act, each one marking Conal's reaction to his subjects' shifty dealings.

"One of the motivations for all art," says Conal, "is that a project means something important, and you hope there's an audience for it. But with *MWNL,* half of it was, 'man, when this thing hits the streets, it's really gonna look cool.'"

Besides looking cool, *MWNL* also reawakened for many the centuries-old art form of political postering, an avenue for editorial comment borne of citizen participation and used historically to reflect political feeling. The act begins in late-night coffee shops, where Conal outlines "guerrilla etiquette" to his crews, clarifying his goals of "counter-infotainment" and empowerment through direct cooperative action. Armed with buckets of glue, cheap brushes, a stack of posters, and a reliable vehicle, they hit the neighborhoods, postering construction sites or abandoned buildings in a zigzag fashion, avoiding private property and, if possible, the police. In his book *Art Attack*, Conal describes a dozen encounters with men in blue, with whom Conal always fully cooperates. Most are interested simply in getting the crews out of their jurisdiction. One LA cop, after hearing Conal's "party line"—that he's involved in a first-amendment art project, a "consciousness-raising, grassroots-citizenship" form of expression—replied: "Let me raise your consciousness, citizen. Get your ass off my beat."

"My art isn't just about politics, it really is politics," Conal says. "Postering is an act of protest, of

minor civil disobedience. The urgency of my subjects' high crimes warrants a speedy response occasionally construed," he smiles, "as a misdemeanor."

Familiarity and notoriety are crucial, and white-collar politicians make good subjects because their likenesses are recognizable. A recent project features GOP leader Robert Dole, Richard Nixon, and the text "Nothing Personal," occasioned by Dole's performance during the "week-long national amnesia" of Nixon's funeral. *Nothing Personal's* three-color starkness and ghastly, wrinkled rendering of "ugly white men" is signature Conal, who's also

the first to admit the limitations of his satirical form.

"My style functions best in a negative way: People tend to look and go, 'Oh, it's another one of that poster guy's things. Who's he dissing now?' instead of, 'Who is that? What's that about?' I think one of the smartest things I could do at this point is create another pictorial style of nonsanctioned public address that didn't look like me."

Conal's desire to branch out led him to *We're All One Color*, a 1989 poster addressing gang wars in South-Central LA; with community members, rappers, and an anti–police brutality group he released *DIS ARM*

a year after Rodney King's verdict; he also designed a second-stage curtain for Lollapalooza. No figure too sacred, he lets slip future plans to poster the Pope, a full-color extravaganza rivaling his Bakker-family diptych *False Profit*. He hints at a work-in-progress entitled *Ghost in the Machine*, a series dedicated to "moments in U.S. history when the spectacle of democracy rears its ugly head."

As Conal himself makes clear, he and other street artists are essentially holding public officials accountable for what they are—or aren't—doing: His slogan is "So many bad guys, so little time." ◆

BURNING MAN

Picture yourself on the largest flat expanse of land in North America, Nevada's Black Rock Desert. Heat waves shimmer off the hardpan alkali flat, and a fine white dust swirls on the wind. Thunderheads gather over the distant mountains that ring the plain, but the sky above you is a deep, cloudless blue. Behind you is your camp, a Rube Goldberg mix of vans, tents, and RVs arranged in a great circle. Scattered across the plain you see other artifacts less easily explained: a giant fiberglass dog head; an enormous, vaguely phallic mud tower. One of your friends has a radio tuned to the local pirate station; like the daily newspaper folded in your pocket, it will exist only for a few short days and then disappear, like

Stuart Mangrum

some exotic desert mushroom. You press an icy bottle to your forehead, savoring the cold, and look up. There above you, tall as a four-story building, stands the strangely graceful human figure known as Burning Man.

Grabbing a rope, you lend a hand as the Man is lowered to the ground. Final preparations are made, and the crowd swells. Costumed dancers lay down a drumbeat as the sky darkens. At last, a signal comes down the line and you haul on your ropes again, raising the Man to his full height, arms outstretched. The drumming intensifies as the sun drops over the horizon, and the Man erupts into flame under a vast and impartial desert sky. One by one the slim neon tubes lining his huge limbs illuminate, and carefully concealed explosives add their staccato thunder to the wild rhythm of many drums. Finally, consumed by fire, he collapses to the desert floor, where the wreckage burns long into the night, a bonfire out of some wild primordial dream.

What does it all *mean?* Feel free to ask, but don't expect the same answer twice. Is it a neo-pagan pyro rave or an avant-garde art festival? A cyberculture summit meeting or a celebration of the forces of nature? A visionary experiment in temporary community or a post-postmodern weenie roast? Or is it just, as a chemistry grad student from Cal Tech told me last year, "One hell of a party"? Nowadays, when people ask me about Burning Man, I just say, "Go."

In the space of a few days, I met a journalist from Switzerland, a journeyman carpenter, two tenured college professors, a pagan masseuse from Santa Barbara, a gang of anarcho-feminist writers from Texas, an unemployed gypsum worker from upstate Nevada, and two sisters from Montana who started an impromptu event in the space between our two cars: molding little human figures out of bread dough and sticking them to bottle rockets, which we then lit and launched. Was it art? Did it mean anything? I don't know, but it sure was fun.

This sort of spontaneous activity is central to the Burning Man experience. Throughout the long weekend people indulge their whims, their fantasies, their creative impulses. If you choose to start something—be it as simple as a card game or as involved as a dada theater piece—someone is bound to join you. Like to dress up in costumes? Fine, bring 'em. Clothes too confining? Likewise, no problem. However you choose to express yourself—through visual art, machine art, poetry, music, dance, whatever—you're encouraged to do so in a non-competitive, cooperative environment where distinctions like "professional" and "amateur," "audience" and "spectator" become meaningless, even absurd.

Burning Man is one of the last places on earth where people from all walks of life, all social strata, and all points of the compass can come together and share an extraordinary experience, a very primal experience: surviving as a group in a challenging environment, creating a temporary culture of their own design, and sharing one of the most elemental experiences of our species, the awesome mystery of fire.

Oh yeah and it's also one hell of a party. ♦

Burning Man has been an annual event since 1986. For more information call the Burning Man hotline at 415/985-7471.

Tyree-Lynch

Joey Skaggs

Andrew Hultkrans

"If you're an artist, you use the medium that communicates the best, and what bigger medium than the media?" asks Joey Skaggs, a practitioner of the rare art of media hoaxing. A trained painter and sculptor, Skaggs found early on that traditional modes of artistic expression were inadequate to broadcast socio-political messages to mass audiences. Since 1966, he's been baiting the press and making asses of journalists with a series of well-publicized hoaxes.

A sampling of his work would have to include the *Cathouse for Dogs*, where Skaggs placed an ad in the *Village Voice* offering "a savory selection of hot bitches, from pedigree (Fifi, the French Poodle) to mutts (Lady the Tramp)" for "dogs only, no weirdos please," resulting in hundreds of calls from loving dog owners hoping to get a "little tail for their dog." The media bought the farm, falling for a staged floor show with female models and provocatively coifed pooches. The ASPCA and the cops weren't far behind, and ABC News ran a documentary with both sides: Joey, as the cruel whoremaster of Manhattan, and the ASPCA doing their best Moral Majority routine. The documentary was nominated for an Emmy, and Joey got subpoenaed by the Attorney General. Skaggs revealed the hoax, as he intended to do, but ABC never retracted their story, nor did they do a follow-up with its source.

The media's failure to give airtime to the intention of the hoax revealed the arrogant irresponsibility of the press corps, and gave Skaggs the blueprint for his later pranks. "First there's the hook, when I do the performance; next, I document the process of miscommunication, or how the media twists the content and meaning of the message; finally, I talk about the serious issues underlying the performance piece. The media often trivialize the third stage by saying 'Oh, he's a hoaxter, he has an

"CAT HOUSE FOR DOGS"
Featuring a savory selection of Hot
Bitches-from pedigree(Fifi the French
Poodle)to mutts(Lady the Tramp)
Handler & Vet on duty-stud & photo
service available-no weird-os,Please
Dogs only-By appt. 212-260-6371

ego problem, he wants attention, etc.' Sometimes they make physical threats. An ego-bruised journalist is not going to see the bigger picture. He's only going to see that I humiliated him or his profession. That's typical of a lot of journalists, because they think they are stars, that they're authorities, that they have the power to mold public opinion, to feed us bullshit. It goes to their heads."

A Skaggs hoax is instantly recognizable (by the initiated) for its bittersweet quality—a deliciously preposterous premise with a sharp aftertaste. In other words, it's funny until one realizes that what is being exposed is quite disturbing. The lingering malodorous smell left behind by a Skaggs hoax reminds us that the media often functions as the propaganda wing of corporate America. "My message is: You're already being pranked every day. If you think *I'm* the prankster, you are sadly mistaken. I'm just ringing the bell."

Later hoaxes include: *Giuseppe Scagolli's Celebrity Sperm Bank*, in which Skaggs offered rock star sperm to the highest bidder (Mick Jagger, Bob Dylan, and Paul McCartney received the most requests); the *Miracle Roach Hormone Pill*, developed by "entomologist Dr. Joseph Gregor of Metamorphosis Institute," which was touted to cure arthritis,

acne, anemia, menstrual cramps, and to make one invulnerable to nuclear radiation; the *Fat Squad*, in which "Joe Bones" and some beefy actors posed as diet-enforcement commandos-for-hire, ready to come live in your home and physically restrain you from eating fattening foods twenty-four hours a day; the *Save the Geoduck* campaign, in which Skaggs, posing as Dr. Richard Long, rallied to save the well-hung clam from Japanese poaching (the Japanese used the geoduck's impressive "leg" as an aphrodisiac, according to Dr. Long); and *Hair Today, Ltd.*, in which Skaggs, as Native American surgeon Dr. Joseph Chenango, advertised a revolutionary hair transplanting method, using the posthumously donated scalps of the freshly dead.

Simultaneously the most humorous and most depressing element of a Skaggs hoax is his ability to regularly dupe the same media organs, despite the use of thematically obvious and sophomoric aliases. Skaggs quickly deflates the assumption that reporters are educated by employing bad Kafka references in a roach pill scam, Dr. Dick Long championing the phallic geoduck, and a Native American scalp surgeon. Skaggs maintains that he includes the screaming clues to maximize his message: that the media are as skeptical

Giuseppe Scaggoli

Director of the Celebrity Spermbank

Jay Jay Skaggs

Hawaii-to-California Windsurfer

Hair Today, Ltd.

as a two-year-old child. "I'm saying 'catch me' and if you don't, you'll be very embarrassed." Although he is caught more often now than in the past, Skaggs continues to successfully flim-flam "respectable" journalists.

Since 1990, he has gone high tech, circulating a well-designed brochure for a "virtual vacation" spa called "Comacocoon." Playing on the public's fears of travel abroad, and their blind faith in technology as personal panacea, the Comacocoon brochure offers a "dream vacation package, which, utilizing our pioneering BioImpression™ computer system, gives you a state of total suspended animation and intensive, concentrated regeneration through anesthesiology and subliminal programming." While you doze through the fantasy of your choice, whether it be the "Magical Mystery Tour" or the "Don Juan," you can also enjoy cosmetic surgery, dentistry, electronic muscle toning, tanning, and language lessons. Engineered by Dr. Joseph Schlafer (German for "sleep"), Comacocoon garnered Skaggs a flurry of press, including overdue coverage of his mission as a hoaxter.

After pausing briefly to issue a bogus memo from Mayor Dinkins's office proposing to auction off the Brooklyn Bridge for civic revenue, Joey married church and state by peddling a portable confession booth outside of the 1992 Democratic National Convention as Father Joseph, a Dominican priest from California. Mounted on a customized bicycle, the elaborate and fully functional *Portofess* and its slogan "Religion on the move for people on the go" made front pages around the nation and appeared on national TV.

Skaggs then trained his sights on the emerging cyberculture and its desperate urge to marry meat with machine. After booking booth space at the Toronto Invention Show under the firm name "Sexonix," Skaggs showed up empty-handed, pretending to be the victim of Canada's prudish customs officials. He staged a press conference in which he claimed to have developed a bona fide virtual sex rig. Some Canadian press bought it, and Skaggs, and his collaged "system demo" videotape (including graphics segments of *Lawnmower Man*) were aired on Canadian TV.

Not willing to stop there, Skaggs took his whiny confiscation story to cyberspace, posting a plea for help on ECHO, Fidonet, and the WELL bulletin boards. Many "wellholes" (as Skaggs calls the users of the Sausalito-based online service), fell for the posting, until one user recognized Skaggs's name from Re/Search's *Pranks!* book, and another grudgingly tracked down his paper trail.

The WELL climate after the "outing" was surprisingly humorless, save for a few prank aficionados. A general log-rolling ensued, with much strutting, feather-puffing, and "you can't fool the WELL" attitude. Skaggs was not surprised by the response. "Any new technology is the artist's territory, and that means lies, satire, disinformation, hoaxes. Shocking those people on the WELL was my goal. They had this mind-set that 'this is my space,' not realizing that it was certainly not their space. BBS users can be a lynch mob. They are very self-righteous, but they're just as gullible and irresponsible as everybody else. Just because they're on a computer doesn't give them brains or an imagination."

While utopian Netheads tout the Internet's "many-to-many" model as a self-correcting, bias-free information organ, Skaggs maintains the Internet is as fallible as the evening news. "The idea of the Internet as a bias-free news source is so gullible, totally unrealistic and against human nature. Any prankster worth his salt is going to do something just to fuck it up. These 'amateur reporters' online have all watched too many cop shows. They all want to be heroes."

Undaunted by his lukewarm BBS experience, Skaggs made his first foray into TV advertising on Hawaii's CNN Headline News affiliates on April 1, 1994. He appeared 40 times over the course of the Fool's Day as "Maqdananda, Psychic Attorney." Surrounded by cheesy New Age paraphernalia, Skaggs played an astral ambulance chaser, asking "Why deal with the legal system without knowing the outcome beforehand? Let me tell you whether to sue or settle, if you'll win or lose. I use nontraditional techniques to determine the outcome of legal decisions." The pitch continued: "Have you ever been the victim of psychic injustice? Are you suffering from psychic surgery malpractice? Do you wish to renegotiate contracts made during past lives?" Although the commercial was his looniest prank to date, Skaggs's voice-mail box at 1-808-UCA-DADA was flooded with calls. "The sad part is that there are people who are willing to suspend their critical judgment to support their own wishful thinking."

One of Skaggs's most recent pranks uncovered something far more disturbing than New Age lemmings, and brought him his most threatening responses ever. In May 1994, he mass-mailed a letter on Korean business letterhead to 1,500 dog shelters around the country. In a scandalous parody of Asian pidgin English, Skaggs, posing as a Mr. Kim Yung Soo, offered to buy spare dogs from the shelters to be used for food. "Dog shelter kill million of dog, cost money. Dog shelter cremate dog, cost money. Dog shelter need money to operate. Where it get money? Hard to get money. Many people like to eat dog. People need to eat dog. Where do they get dog? Some people they raise dog to eat. Some steal dog, make some people angry. That not right. We like make proposal to your dog shelter to sell us dog. You save money, you make money. We buy all dog, regardless of size and color. No burn up dog. No waste dog. People pet no disappear. Everybody happy. Dog no suffer. We have quick death for dog."

During the following week, Skaggs received thousands of outraged calls, faxes, and letters all taking the proposal at face value. Some people offered to sell him dogs, although Skaggs believed these were vigilante attempts at entrapment. "The people who tried to sell me dog wanted to be heroes: [*redneck accent*] 'Ahh, they're just fucking Koreans. We'll call him up, sell him 400 pounds of dog, bust him, and we'll be on *Hee-rald-o*!'" Most of the communications were hostile, many threatening to murder Skaggs's Korean alias and other Asians indiscriminately. Racist slurs abounded, from "your dirty little Asian babies" to "filthy yellow devil" to "How about Asian stew? Asian hands a specialty." Skaggs was appalled, though not entirely surprised, by the bashing.

"If I were Hindu, I'd believe that cows are sacred. A cow could be the reincarnation of my grandmother! So if you eat McDonald's in my face, it doesn't show a lot of respect for my culture. But if I say, 'Hey, dog is good to eat, too,' Americans are like 'What do you mean, dog?!? Fuck you, man!' The dog meat hoax was a good example of cultural intolerance and racism. I got calls that would make you fear for your life."

Having forgotten the *Cathouse for Dogs* years earlier, the ASPCA got into the act again, issuing a press release denouncing the letter as a "cruel hoax with racist overtones," but not before many news outlets covered the letter as straight news. Skaggs was particularly disappointed with the media's lack of follow-up on the dog meat hoax. "The media never went to the source. They never cared about my intent. They also did a total denial of reality. I mean, what happens to those millions of dogs who nobody takes home? Who puts them to sleep? The ASPCA had its own image to uphold, and the media was totally manipulated."

The dog meat hoax further illustrated the Brit theory that Americans are immune to irony. "The role of the satirist needs to be played more. I did the dog meat hoax with Jonathan Swift's 'A Modest Proposal' in mind, but most people don't have a sense of humor, or are illiterate." Skaggs's reservations aside, as an "outing" of current anti-Korean paranoia, the prank worked beautifully.

One would be foolish to trust him, but Skaggs claims he's going to lay low for a while. He refused to take credit for the nuptial merger of Michael Jackson and Lisa Marie Presley. He did admit, however, that he has been working for two years on a slick, high-tech prank with a computer graphics artist of "Oscar caliber." Stay tuned. ◆

Stickers designed by
Ward Parkway

Enlarge/Reduce as needed. Color photocopy onto pressure-sensitive paper and trim out. Subvertise your world with stickers!

The Urban Absurdist Survival Kit™

TOOLS NEEDED:

X-acto knife

or scissors

Stickyback paper

Ruler

Copy machine

Every day, we are inundated with signs and labels telling us what to buy, how to park, who to see, and where to go. Normal people enjoy being told what to do, and this trait provides an excellent opportunity for playful mischief.

The Urban Absurdist Survival Kit™ has been specially designed to make city living a fresh experience. Use a color photocopier to reproduce the labels onto stickyback paper (available at art and stationery shops) and post them in places inhabited by rigid, authoritarian droids. The stickers will amuse folks who appreciate a good joke and confuse or even anger stuffed shirts who have no tolerance for fun.

The International Press Association (Congratulations! You're now a member!) badge can be used to gain entrance to all sorts of events from which you'd normally be excluded for lack of credentials or money. The Attention Deficit Receipt can be issued to officious time-wasters: bureaucrats, salespeople, religious zealots, etc.

Don't limit yourself to this starter kit, though. The best stickers will be the ones you make to turn an especially dull situation into a riot. ♦

DISCLAIMER:
For Entertainment Purposes Only. Do not ingest without first consulting your physician. Not responsible for lost or stolen goods, damage to property or to tunnel realities resulting from application of these stickers. Use kit at your own risk.

▼ Print lots of copies of this one and spread the Happy Mutant virus!

EVOLVE

SUPPORT MUTATION

SURVIVAL OF ANY SPECIES OVER TIME DEPENDS ON RESERVES OF MUTANTS CAPABLE OF EXPLOITING OR RESISTING OPPORTUNITIES

DANGER

INFO HAZARD

CONTAINS VIRULENT INFORMATION
PROGRAMMED TO DISPLACE/BLOCK CONCEPTS
CRUCIAL TO SIMIAN BRAIN EVOLUTION

INSANE

UNQUESTIONING HIERARCHICAL AUTOMATONS

INTELLECTUAL CAUTION ADVISED

CAUTION

SMALL MIND SECTOR

DISPLAYS OF ENLIGHTENMENT MAY
CARRY RISKS FOR INDIVIDUALS

BOREDOM

EXTREMELY DULL

SELF-ENTERTAINMENT NECESSARY
FOR MAINTAINING CONSCIOUSNESS

Why only have warning stickers that deal with physical peril? Remind your co-workers that their brains may be in grave danger if they don't heed these warnings.

Color photocopy onto pressure-sensitive paper and trim out.

NOTICE
HUMOR NOT APPRECIATED
SERIOUSNESS MANDATORY AT ALL TIMES
CYNICISM, IRONY, AND ABSURDITY WILL BE PROSECUTED TO THE FULLEST EXTENT POSSIBLE

SUBMIT
CONFORMITY MANDATORY
YOU MUST TOE THE PARTY LINE
ATTEMPTS AT ORIGINAL THOUGHT OR ACTION WILL RESULT IN SEVERE AND IMMEDIATE CONSEQUENCES

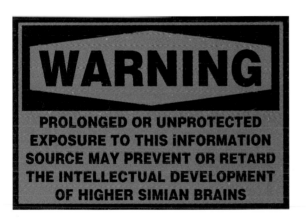

WARNING
PROLONGED OR UNPROTECTED EXPOSURE TO THIS iNFORMATION SOURCE MAY PREVENT OR RETARD THE INTELLECTUAL DEVELOPMENT OF HIGHER SIMIAN BRAINS

PRIMITIVE
THIS AREA HAS BEEN FOUND INHOSPITABLE TO BIPEDAL BEINGS DEMONSTRATING INDIVIDUALITY AND/OR OTHER EVOLVED BEHAVIOR

SURGEON ADMIRAL'S WARNING: Conformity Causes Unconsciousness, Boredom, And May Lead To A Persistant Vegetative Dream-State.

STURGEON GENERAL'S WARNING: Smoking This Combustible Substance Will Result In Absolutely No Psychedelic Perceptual Shift.

Reduce these food package warnings to fit your favorite grocery items.

100% RECYCLED FOOD PRODUCT
GUARANTEED TO MEET OR EXCEED HUMAN EDIBILITY STANDARDS
K78.394003   UASK INTERNATIONAL STANDARDS HB8.14-S 1994

CONTAMINATED GOODS
FOR SALE TO CODE-LEVEL MAGENTA HUMANS ONLY
REMOVE THIS LABEL BEFORE DISPLAYING

FUN FOOD
FOR RECREATIONAL CONSUMPTION ONLY
THIS EDIBLE SUBSTANCE CONTAINS ABSOLUTELY NO NUTRITIONAL VALUE
WORLD NUTRITION COUNCIL   WNC IDENTIFICATION PLACARD - B438.90 REV. 1992

▲ Imagine the Normals in your neighborhood trying to figure out what this one means.

▼ Why should orthodox Jews have all the Kosher food fun? Place these labels on foodstuffs and other products that Catholics buy (Marshmallow Creme, white bread, Mayonnaise, Mother Mary votive candles, Pope on a Rope, etc.).

BIOENGINEERED FOOD PRODUCT
GENETICALLY-ALTERED THROUGH COMBINATION WITH HUMAN DNA
GH4.836678   UASK INTERNATIONAL STANDARDS XT5.1425K 1994

APPROVED BY THE POPE
CATHOLIC COSHER

Color photocopy onto pressure-sensitive paper and trim out.

▼ Enlarge to business card size. Add photo and signature. Laminate one copy to wear and put one in your wallet. The world is the oyster of the press!

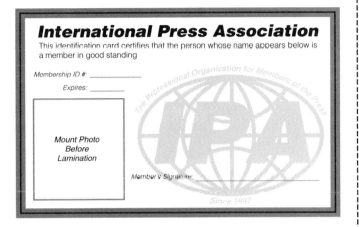

International Press Association

This identification card certifies that the person whose name appears below is a member in good standing

Membership ID #: _____

Expires: _____

Mount Photo
Before
Lamination

The Professional Organization for Members of the Press

IPA

Member's Signature _____

Since 1897

COMPLIES WITH INTERNATIONAL

CLASS B EMISSION STANDARDS

ATTENTION DEFICIT RECEIPT

This receipt shall serve as a legal record for any transaction involving the involuntary deduction of attention currency (i.e.: wasting someone's time)

Name _____

...*has increased my individual Attention Deficit by:* _____

☐ Seconds ☐ Days
☐ Minutes ☐ Months
☐ Hours ☐ Years

Description of Transaction

Time: ___ : ___ : ___ ☐ AM ☐ PM

Signed _____ Date _____

Print on parchment or NCR-type paper. Award to worthy bores and motor mouths. ▲

CRAIG BALDWIN:

PLAGIARISM SAVES TIME

Will Kreth

It's a Sunday night in San Francisco. A benefit film festival for filmmaker Craig Baldwin is under way at a scrappy little film and video collective called Artist's Television Access (or just ATA). The crowd's come, not only to see a melange of short clips and videos, but to bask in the light of a man whose cult following reaches far beyond his Mission District haunts. Up in the projection room, Baldwin, a manic of the moving image, is at the controls. He's at home here because ATA's literally his home (he lives upstairs and edits his films in the basement during all-night canned cappuccino jags). The audience is seated in mismatched rows of old movie theater seats that look like they've been wrestled out of dumpsters.

Not only do the seats come from dumpsters, but much of Baldwin's best footage is found in trash cans containing film somebody else threw away. After studying under found-footage auteur Bruce Conner at San Francisco State University, Baldwin, 43, vibrantly reinvented the found-footage genre and has taken it to a new vantage point for cultural commentary and critique. *Tribulation 99*, Baldwin's pseudo-documentary tour de farce of subterranean alien invaders—disguised as South and Central American Marxist revolutionaries—is a cult classic for discriminating midnight movie aficionados.

Baldwin's latest film, *Sonic Outlaws*, rips into current cultural hot-button issues such as copyright, plagiarism, and the "fair use" of copyright-protected material. Using his own collage aesthetic to comment on the collage works of his contemporaries, *Sonic Outlaws* showcases a series of interviews with such audio/visual anarchists as Negativland, John Oswald, Emergency Broadcast Network, Doug Kahn, and the Tape Beatles.

An uncommonly hyperkinetic personality for being a left coaster (born in Oakland, raised in Sacramento, and a San Francisco resident for nearly two decades), Baldwin both thinks and speaks at several miles-a-minute. A conversation on philosophy or film theory can (and often does) go on for hours. Extremely literate, Baldwin considers himself "an adversarial artist."

"I have this—I don't know if *perverse* is the word—kind of Beat aesthetic that wants to go 'against the grain'—not jumping on the 'Cyberpunk' or 'Rock 'n' Roll' bandwagons and just throwing out every cliché in the book. My point is the *surprise*." ◆

Bart Nagel

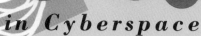

S h e n a n i g a n s
in Cyberspace

Gareth Branwyn

If you have access to the Internet and USENET newsgroups, you can join a constant twittering prankster's think tank in the alt.shenanigans newsgroup. The group was originally formed as a place to discuss harmless practical jokes. The founders of the newsgroup wanted to differentiate between pranks that were destructive and malicious and those that were only intended to confuse or fool the victim. Lighthearted, good-natured naughtiness is the general idea of shenanigans. Of course, postings to a public forum like alt.shenanigans cannot be controlled, but it's nice to know that those who started the newsgroup had a noble mission.

What actually does get posted to the group varies widely from the tried and true (and now boring) dorm pranks like short-sheeting beds, egging cars, and putting Saran Wrap on toilets to some very clever and funny acts of poetic terrorism. Here's a brief sampling:

Shopping for Others

When someone leaves their shopping cart unattended in the supermarket, hide stuff in it that they would NEVER buy. Try to assess their likes and dislikes. If they look like a vegetarian, hide some calves' livers. If they look like the Hungry Man Dinner type, tuck some tofu and sprouts under their Cheez Whiz and Ding Dongs. Then position yourself so that you can watch their baffled reactions and explanations at the checkout counter. (Attributed to film director John Waters)

Fax Maintenance

Here's a fun prank to play on someone you want to annoy at their job. Make an official-looking fax transmittal form. Something like this:

Universal Fax Maintenance

A free service of the American Facsimile Machine Association

The AFMA maintains a free-of-charge industry-wide fax machine maintenance call service. According to our records (based on date of purchase information provided by the manufacturer and/or place-of-purchase), your fax machine is now due for a toner refill.

If you do not attend to this immediately, you could damage your machine. To verify that the machine is indeed low on fax toner, please check the toner indicator lamp. To do this, lift up the top cover of your machine and look under the paper roll housing. You should see a red blinking light if the machine needs a toner refill. If you can't find the indicator lamp, consult the manufacturer's manual or call your service provider.

We hope that this automated service call has been a big help to you and that your machine, after being properly refilled, will give you years of reliable performance.

(Of course, fax machines do not require "toner refills" and there is no "toner indicator lamp," so this should keep your mark busy for a while. Make sure that your fax phone number does not appear on the fax that you send out.)

The Telemarketer's Game

Why let those pesky phone sales people ruin your dinner? Now you can turn their annoying calls into a fun and challenging game that the whole family can play! Tabulate your scores and post 'em to alt.shenanigans.

Scoring:

Basic Point System:
- For each minute spent on the phone 10 pts.
- Getting transferred to someone

G.R.

who makes more than minimum wage 15 pts

- For each minute spent on the phone with person making more than minimum wage 25 pts

Bonus Points:

- Getting them to repeat part of the "script" 5 pts
- Getting answers to stupid questions 5 pts
- Changing the subject 50 pts
- Making the salesperson angry 175 pts
- Making the salesperson use profanity 750 pts
- Getting the boss on the phone and telling them the salesperson used profanity 1,500 pts
- Getting their 1-800 number 10 pts
- Posting their 1-800 number to alt.sex as a free "Phone Sex" line 50 pts
- Checking the number a week later and finding it busy or disconnected 5,000 pts

Subway and Elevator Shenanigans

1. Giggle the whole time you're reading a book. Especially a phone book.

2. Bring a little radio and listen to radio static only.

3. Bring a Chia pet in on a leash and talk to it, pet it, and kiss it. Worship it in public.

4. Bring a Mr. Potato Head and create a face while looking at someone and nodding approvingly.

5. Get four to five friends to dress up in totally different outfits, say: a businessperson, a bike messenger, a homeless person, a semi-white-collar yuppie type, a blue-collar sweatshirt type. Each gets on separately, looking as though they are complete strangers. One person starts humming, then quietly singing, a tune. The singing gets louder and one of the other shensters joins in, as if spontaneously, until, by the middle of the song, everyone is singing. You really score points if you can get others to join in.

Another Elevator Shen

When I was in Nanjing, China, I did a fun elevator trick. The elevator had the floor number buttons like this:

19	20
17	18
15	16
13	14
11	12
etc.	

They were easily removable, and replaceable. Late one night, I changed them to:

20	19
18	17
16	15
14	13
12	11
etc.	

I then changed the big floor number signs that hung on the walls opposite the elevator doors on each floor to correspond appropriately with the new floor numbering designations. Each floor in the building was virtually identical, with rooms numbered 1 through 20, no floor number, on each floor. Mass confusion.

Missing Pet Shen

Make up a poster about the lost light of your life.

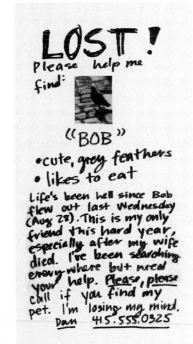

To access alt.shenanigans, you need to be on the USENET newsgroups. The alt.shenanigans FAQ is stored at the alt.shenanigans archive at elf.tn.cornell.edu as /shenanigans/shenanigans-faq. ◆

How to Work at Work

John Shirley

What could be more seditious than doing your own work at work? I don't mean leaning out the window to sell hot dogs to the exec in the company on the floor below. I mean maybe developing your own software at work. Or writing a novel—that's what I did, on the extremely rare occasions I held a real job.

How to get away with it? Here's how I did it. First of all, I brought my own computer to work. "Used to it," I said. "More efficient on it. Can't learn that other system." This way, you see, they couldn't snoop into my files so easily.

Suppose you're writing another one of these dreadful screenplays that everyone thinks they ought to write. If you work in a cubicle kind of office where another maze-rat can suddenly turn up and surprise you, you need to set things up so your screen is hidden by your body. The next rule in hiding the screenplay from the boss and his subsets is SAVE SAVE SAVE. Save your text by reflex, constantly, neurotically, even up to every finished sentence. That way, if you've got to cut out of the file fast before someone spots what's on the screen, you only lose a few words.

And "fast" is the operative word. You've got to have a special set of reflexes for this act of subversion and time-pilfering. You've got to know exactly where the file you're supposed to be working on is—and how to get there with, ideally, two keystrokes. There's software where you can have "notes" hidden in the file that you can buzz to in a second—something that looks like Official Work. Or you can just get out of the file fast and act as if you're in transition from one office file to another. Got to be very casual about it, fast but smooth in your motions, so they don't smell fear.

Your file names have to be neutral, chosen for their apparent work-related qualities—but they're code for what you're really working on.

You can work on floppy disks, of course, so that nothing is in evidence on the company's hard drive. Make sure some portion of your desk is messy—if you're a neat freak, make it a drawer—so the offending disks can be hidden in apparent disarray. Apparent disarray hides a great deal. Create a persona of "good worker but a little spacey"—then they'll cut you slack.

You're a human virus, you understand, infiltrating the cell that is your business and using its reproductive proteins for your own creative DNA. Your "receptors" must seem authentic.

Penetrate—and reproduce! ◆

Cacophony Society

Julie Fishman

"We don't accept the entertainment that's spoon fed to us through TV and other commercial media," says Cacophony Society member Maxwell Maude. The tall, silver-haired Maude has a perpetual mysterious smile and eyes that twinkle with imminent mischief. "We want to create our own entertainment and our own experiences."

Do-it-yourself entertainment, Cacophony style, might mean dressing up in formal wear at midnight for a candlelit stroll through the sewers of Oakland. Or it might mean putting on clown suits and waiting at different bus stops along a city line, just to bewilder the passengers when they see one clown at each stop board the bus, oblivious to the other orange wigs and red rubber noses.

While costumed events make up a large part of the leaderless Cacophony Society's fun (who could pass up "Cavemen Go to Rodeo Drive Day"?), sometimes they just operate on pure nerve and a sense of the absurd. Not too long ago, Cacophony's LA chapter bought a booth at the annual G.I. Joe collectors' convention and set up a display of the tiny plastic fighting men in various states of dismemberment, crucifixion, and sexual deviance. They brought along a video camera to tape the angry G.I. Joe militants who smashed their display to bits. "LA is Cacophony's most confrontational chapter," says San Francisco member Sebastian Melmouth, the society's Chairman of Responsibility Avoidance. "Every chapter has its own flavor." There are four chapters: San Francisco (the original), Los Angeles, Portland, and Seattle. New York is next on the hit list.

A year after the Cacophony Society held their John Wayne Bobbitt memorial weenie roast, they made hundreds of severed latex penises and packaged them as chew toys for pet dogs, under the "Laughing Bitch" brand name. They sent the products to all the chapters with instructions for members to smuggle the chew toy penises onto shelves at supermarkets. When shoppers saw them for "sale," they were delighted. The bar code printed on the label caused the purchase to show up on the register receipt as "chicken sausage." Store clerks were either amused, mystified, or angered by the prank.

Cacophony, started in 1986, likes to collaborate with other groups, such as the Weird Car people, Survival Research Labs, the Church of Elvis, and Burning Man. They are nonprofit, nonreligious, and nonpolitical, mainly because the members all have different religious and political beliefs and don't want to prevent anyone from joining.

If you think this sounds like fun, then congratulations—you're already a member! For information about Cacophony, their mailing list, creating an event, or even starting your own chapter, call the branch nearest you: San Francisco: 415/665-0351, Los Angeles: 213/937-2759, Portland: 503/232-3504, Seattle: 206/521-1185. ◆

BUILDING HACKERS

Simson L. Garfinkel

"NO TOAD SEXING ALLOWED"

I first saw this prohibition against scrutinizing amphibian genitalia in a stairwell at the Massachusetts Institute of Technology. The message was written in thick black Magic Marker in the basement of the Chemistry Building. Around it were dozens of other symbols, names, and messages that had collected over the years. The writing wasn't quite graffiti. It was more like nerd-tagging: black-and-white proof that the hackers whose names littered the wall had been there, in late night or early morning, and had left their mark. (The hackers call these tags "sign-ins.")

That was all very well and good, but what was that same "NO TOAD SEXING ALLOWED" decree doing here, inside a ventilation shaft on the fourth floor of a research lab at the

Weizmann Institute of Science, in Rehovot, Israel?

On the other hand, what was I doing in a ventilation shaft? Just call it hacker curiosity, I guess.

Long before there were computer hackers, there was a generation of hackers of another kind. Call them "building hackers." Like their cyber-space descendants, these hackers lived to discover new places; to find their ways into the most hidden nooks and crannies; to learn for themselves how things worked around them, and then manipulate their physical sur-roundings to do their bidding. It's a more physical, more athletic form of computer hacking, where it's just as important to be smart and courageous as it is to be in good shape—and where the risks of getting caught are very real and always present.

All the aspiring building hacker

needs to get started is a sense of the possible (and a building to hack, of course). Next time you're in a large building with some time on your hands, take the elevator to the basement. Once you're there, look around. Explore. Surreptitiously try a few doorknobs. When you find one that's unlocked—and nobody's around—take a look inside. If you find a flight of stairs going down to the sub-basement, follow them, my friend, for they'll lead you to the jackpot.

The most interesting contraptions are waiting around for discovery in sub-basements. Usually, the first thing you'll notice is the ventilation equip-ment: Big fans and compressors; air filters the size of a VW microbus; and air conduits large enough to house a family of four are the norm in most large office buildings. Look further and you'll discover the building's electrical and telephone distribution closets. Don't be intimidated by signs that say "Danger, 13,800 Volts" or "Do not operate radios in this area." On the other hand, don't be stupid either: If you die down in a building's bowels, you have nobody to blame but yourself

Roofs offer many rewards that can't be found in subterranean passageways. First of all, there is the view once you've found your way to the outside. Then there is the implicit danger of the drop to street level. If you've picked a building that's tall enough, you are likely to find an interesting collection of radio transmitters and microwave dishes to ogle. For all these reasons, roofs are generally better defended than basements against unauthorized visits. Before opening a door, scan it carefully for wires or other signs of alarm systems. Check the door after you open it as well: Frequently, sensors are "hidden" inside doorjambs. If you trip an alarm, don't panic: just close the door and calmly walk away.

As you become an experienced hacker, you'll find yourself seeking out the unusual. Every building has its own personality: It's up to you to find it. In Boston's theater district, there's an entire network of underground tunnels connecting the area's oldest buildings. Find them and admire yourself in the ornate 19th-century mirrors that line their walls. In New York City, you can spend your Sundays scoping out abandoned subway stations, but be careful of the mole people—some of them can

be violent. In Chicago, of course, there is the great network of underground chambers and tunnels that flooded several years ago, shutting down the city.

Some of the most rewarding places you will discover are the corners, chambers, and secret passageways that aren't supposed to exist at all: secret rooms that have been walled off, stairways leading to nowhere, entire basements accessible only by forgotten shafts. Bring along your flashlight and your Magic Marker: when you find these rooms, sign in with your hacker handle and the date. The fewer names you find on the wall, the better your skill; you get extra bonus points if you are the first to discover your particular vault or crypt.

A lot of novice hackers ask me, "What do you do if you get caught?"

"I don't know," I tell them. "I've never been caught."

It's the truth. Oh, sure, I was yelled at by the police one Fourth of July when I was climbing on a bridge to get a better view of the fireworks. But generally, when I'm in my element, it's very easy to avoid discovery.

For starters, always have an alibi ready at hand. Pretending that you are lost is an excellent cover. You might be walking in a basement and all of a sudden you come across a suspicious janitor. Just put on the most confused expression you can manage and say, "Excuse me, can you tell me how to get out of here? I have no idea how I got here. I'm looking for the subway station."

It's much easier to pull this off if your Magic Marker and flashlight are out of sight.

Walk slowly and deliberately. Never run. With each step, be alert: Do you hear any other footsteps? Can you hear people talking, or doors slamming shut? Make as little noise as possible, and always be on the lookout for good hiding places. Be prepared to stay hidden for an hour or more if you need to.

Always leave lights and doors the way you find them. Most basements at MIT, for example, have their lights left on. The steam tunnels under Wellesley College, on the other hand, have their lights turned off. With few exceptions, locked doors should be left locked. One exception is doors to the roof: leave these unlocked as a courtesy to other hackers who might follow in your tracks.

Finally, always follow the cardinal rule of hacking: do no harm. Don't break windows, kick in doors, or take a pipewrench to a stubborn lock. Whatever you do, don't steal anything. After all, you're an explorer, not a petty thief.

A final note about sign-ins. Keep them small and inconspicuous—don't cover the walls with funky tags. (If you do, they'll probably be painted over, and you'll get the building custodians peeved.) And come up with something other than "NO TOAD SEXING ALLOWED"— that sign-in has already been taken. ◆

Hacking

Rudy Rucker

No section on reality hacking would be complete without a screed about computer programming, the original form of hacking. This essay is by Rudy Rucker, a contributor to the Great Work of the third millennium: building machines that are alive.

—editors

"Hacking is like building a scale-model cathedral out of toothpicks, except that if one toothpick is out of place the whole cathedral will disappear. And then you have to feel around for the invisible cathedral, trying to figure out which toothpick is wrong. Debuggers make it a little easier, but not much, since a truly screwed-up cutting-edge program is entirely capable of screwing up the debugger as well, so that then it's like you're feeling around for the missing toothpick with a stroke-crippled claw-hand.

"But, ah, the dark dream beauty of the hacker grind against the hidden wall that only you can see, the wall that only you wail at, you the programmer, with the brand new tools that you make up as you go along, your special new toothpick lathes and jigs and your realtime scrimshaw shaver, you alone in the dark with your wonderful tools."

—The Hacker and the Ants,
Rudy Rucker

On a good day, I think of hacking as a tactile experience, like reaching into a tub of clay and kneading and forming the material into the shapes of my desires.

A computer program is a virtual machine that you build by hand. Hacking is like building a car by building all of the parts in the car individually. The good thing is that you have full control, the bad thing is that the process can take so much longer than you expect it to. Are you sure you feel like stamping out a triple-0 z-ring gasket? And compositing the plastic from which to make the gasket? The hacker says, "Yaar! Sounds like fun!"

Of course it does get easier as you build more and more. Often as not, you can reuse old pieces of code that you hacked for other projects. A hacker develops a nice virtual garage of "machine parts" that he or she can reuse. As a beginner, you start out using prefab parts made by others, but sooner or later, you're likely to grit on down to the lowest machine levels to see just how those parts really work.

To be a writer you need something you want to write about; to be a hacker you need something to hack about. You need to have an obsession, a vision that you want to turn into a novel, or into a virtual machine. It's going to take you so long to finish that you will need a fanatic's obsession to see a big project through. Essential in either case is the simple act of not giving up, of going back into it over and over again.

I think the most interesting hacks are programs that turn the computer into a window to a different reality. Programs which express true computer nature. Chaos, fractals, artificial life, cellular automata, genetic algorithms, virtual reality, hyperspace—these are lovely areas that the computer can see into.

I once heard a hacker say, "We are like Leuwenhoek with the microscope. We are peering into new worlds." In an odd way, the most interesting worlds can be found when this new "microscope" looks at itself, perhaps entering a chaotic feedback loop that can close in on some strange attractor.

There are, of course, lame-butts who think hacking means grubbing scraps of information about war and money. What a joke. That's like imagining drugs are for making you a better salesman, or for losing weight. Drugs are for seeing God, and hacking is for delving into the hidden machinery of the universe.

The universe? Didn't I just say that the coolest hacks are in some sense centered on an investigation of what the computer itself can do? Yes, but the computer is a model of the universe.

Sometimes schizos think the universe is a computer—in a bad kind of way—that everything is gray and controlled, and distant numbers are being read off in a monotone, and somewhere a supervisor is tabulating your ever-more-incriminating list of sins.

But in reality, the universe is like a parallel computer, a computer with no master program, a computer filled with self modifying code and autonomous processes—a space of computation, if you will. A good hack can capture this on a simple color monitor. The self-mirroring screen becomes an image of the world at large. As above, so below.

The correspondence between computers and reality changes the way you understand the world. Once you know about fractals, clouds and plants don't look the same. Once you've seen chaotic vibrations on a screen, you recognize them in the waving of tree branches and in the wandering of the media's eye. Cellular automata show how social movements can emerge from individual interactions. Virtual reality instructs you in the beauty of an overhead flock of birds. Artificial life and genetic algorithms let intelligent processes self-organize amidst brute thickets of random events. Hyperspace programs let you finally see into the fourth dimension enough to recognize kinky inside-out reversals as part and parcel of your potentially infinite brain.

Hacking teaches that the secret of the universe need not be so very complex, provided that the secret is set down in a big enough space of computation equipped with feedback and parallelism. Feedback means having a program take its last output as its new input. Parallelism means letting the same program run at many different sites. The universe's physics is the same program running in parallel everywhere, repeatedly updating itself on the basis of its current computation. Your own psychology is a parallel process endlessly revising itself.

Hacking is a yoga, but not an easy one. How do you start? Taking a course in the C programming language is probably the best way to start; or you might independently buy a C compiler and work through the manual's examples. And then find a problem that is your own, something you really want to see, whether it's chaos or whether it's just a tic-tac-toe program. And then start trying to make your vision come to life. The computer will help to show you the way, especially if you pay close attention to your error messages, use the help files—and read the fuckin' manual. It's a harsh yoga; it's a path to mastery. ♦

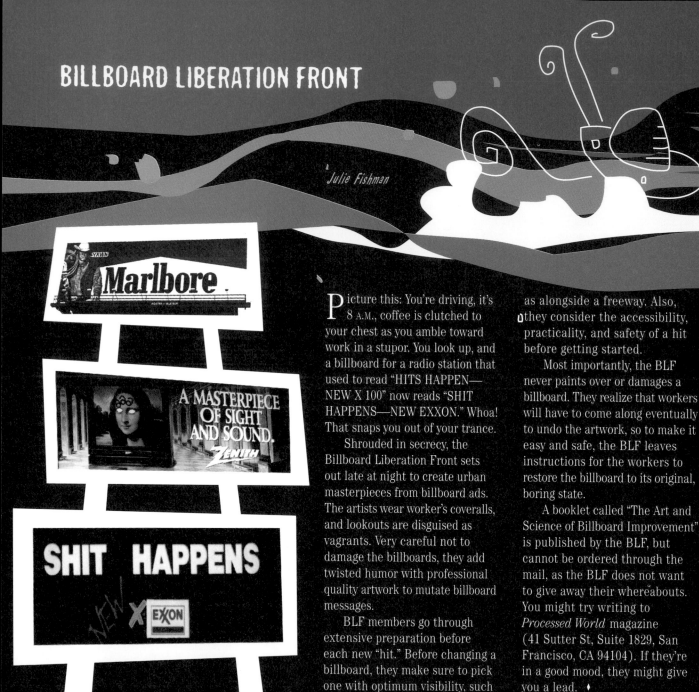

Julie Fishman

Picture this: You're driving, it's 8 A.M., coffee is clutched to your chest as you amble toward work in a stupor. You look up, and a billboard for a radio station that used to read "HITS HAPPEN— NEW X 100" now reads "SHIT HAPPENS—NEW EXXON." Whoa! That snaps you out of your trance.

Shrouded in secrecy, the Billboard Liberation Front sets out late at night to create urban masterpieces from billboard ads. The artists wear worker's coveralls, and lookouts are disguised as vagrants. Very careful not to damage the billboards, they add twisted humor with professional quality artwork to mutate billboard messages.

BLF members go through extensive preparation before each new "hit." Before changing a billboard, they make sure to pick one with optimum visibility, such

as alongside a freeway. Also, they consider the accessibility, practicality, and safety of a hit before getting started.

Most importantly, the BLF never paints over or damages a billboard. They realize that workers will have to come along eventually to undo the artwork, so to make it easy and safe, the BLF leaves instructions for the workers to restore the billboard to its original, boring state.

A booklet called "The Art and Science of Billboard Improvement" is published by the BLF, but cannot be ordered through the mail, as the BLF does not want to give away their whereabouts. You might try writing to *Processed World* magazine (41 Sutter St, Suite 1829, San Francisco, CA 94104). If they're in a good mood, they might give you a lead. ◆

Notes

Better Living Through Silicon

Computers bore Happy Mutants. They do a half-assed job at sending signals to your eyes and ears, while the real world can send ultra-high resolution data to *all* of your senses. So why is everybody sitting around in front of these lousy boxes all day, staring at blocky pictures and typing out chunky-looking text?

Beats us. Maybe it gives them a feeling of accomplishment: "Look, I just updated our recipe card database, balanced the checkbook, and planned our schedules for the next six months!"

Barf. Licking a car's door handle in sub-zero weather sounds like more fun. The only time we get excited about sitting in front of a computer is when we're using it to look through a window into another universe.

There are two kinds of computer universes that excite Happy Mutants at the moment. One is the virtual community of people scattered all across the planet, connecting with each other using their computers and the phone system. If you've ever been on a computer bulletin board, you've recognized the sense of "place" you get when you're inside a virtual community. You aren't just sitting at a table in your room, you're sharing yourself with people from all over the world and helping to create a new kind of social space. The other great thing about virtual communities is that there are tens of thousands of 'em in cyberspace. You're sure to find at least one that's full of people you like, people who'll entertain you and teach you something.

The other type of digital universe we groove on is simulations in which the computer runs a program written to behave like a real-world ecosystem. The term most people use for this is Artificial Life, or a-life for short.

Many a-life programs are so good at taking on lives of their own that they surprise the people that coded them in the first place. This is cool! These programs are novelty engines that any Happy Mutant can set up in his or her room to crank away and generate astonishing new worlds to ponder.

Computer-based worlds may still be poor substitutes for the organic world, but they offer fascinating possibilities and insights into digital worlds to come. "Better Living Through Silicon" covers people who are building simulated universes, and people who are using computers to change the real universe as well. ◆

Chap Wass

your.name @ here

E-MAIL IDENTITY HACKING

Sean Carton

E ver wonder just how those little pranksters manage to send e-mail messages that look like they're coming from the Prez himself? Would you like to send a prank message to your friend and keep your identity a secret? It's easy—here's how! (Type everything as indicated.)

1. Telnet to port 25 on some Internet site:

telnet <site.site.site> 25

2. Port 25 is where the SMTP (Simple Mail Transport Protocol) mail server lives. Your job is to fool the SMTP into thinking that you're another server. First, say hello and tell 'em where you are (not) from:

HELO <your.fake.domain>

3. Next, tease SMTP with a fake e-mail address . . .

MAIL FROM:
<your.fake.name@your.fake.domain>

4. Now that you've introduced yourself, tell SMTP where you want to send your little note:

RCPT TO: <whoever.you.are.sending.it.to@
their.domain>

5. Now, type DATA to let the SMTP server know that you've got a message coming.

6. That was easy! Now, the message:

From:
<your.fake.name@your.fake.domain>
To: <whoever>

<body of message here>

7. When you're done typing, put a period on a line by itself and hit return.

8. All done? Type QUIT to quit. ◆

jorja

NET.BOZO
FIELD GUIDE

Gareth Branwyn

Cyberspace has become so populated that just about every stripe of human is now represented, from working stiffs to Hollywood celebrities. From maw and paw to ABC and MTV. With this surging growth comes a vast array of jerks, idiots, and nincompoops. There are the new people who don't know how to "drive," recklessly careening down the information highway. Or there are the crotchety ol' geezers who bite the heads off the vulnerable newcomers. Commercial opportunists are lurking in the shadows, waiting to unearth new trends, product ideas, and tomorrow's headlines, while shut-in perverts drool over digital dirty pictures and try to virtually molest Net-surfing teenagers.

The following field guide has been prepared by our crack staff of A-I agents who've traversed the vastness of the Net, hunting down the biggest bozos and recording their behaviors and habitats. Xerox and cut these ID cards out, and keep them by your computer when you're online. These days, you never know who (or what) you might run into. ◆

newbie

Description:	First timer. Timid. Quick to misunderstand text-based communication. Flushed with net enthusiasm. Trips over virtual feet a lot. Makes you HATE emoticons :-(
Tech:	AOL e-mail address, uses Performa system bought on Sears credit card. Finds the America Online Tour Guide (at 400 pages) indispensable.
Strengths:	Still has a life offline. Can answer daily e-mail in one sitting.
Weaknesses:	Thinks the MAKE.MONEY.FAST postings might be worth looking into.
Special Powers:	USENET firestarter. Can set off flames by the mere posting of his/her e-mail address.
Alliances:	Floodgaters
Quote:	(In a Chat Room called Hot Gifs) "Hi all. Why isn't anyone talking in here?"
Favorite Cyber Hangout:	Romance Connection on AOL.

knowbot

Description:	Been there—done that. Knows EVERYTHING about everything . . . or at least acts like it. Always condescending. Likes to eat Newbies for breakfast.
Tech:	Sun Workstation, T1 Internet connection. Claims to have taught Ed Kroll everything he knows about the Net.
Strengths:	Exhaustive source of completely useless net.arcana.
Weaknesses:	Pathological inability to comprehend irony or sarcasm. Takes a playful nudge way too seriously.
Special Powers:	Can crush another user's enthusiasm in nanoseconds. "Oh . . . I've known about that system for AGES. I helped beta test it."
Alliances:	Net.Spiders
Quote:	"You idiot! Read the Fucking Manual!!"
Favorite Cyber Hangout:	alt.answers, Experts on the Well.

Bye-Bye Bozo!

Mark Frauenfelder

Every day, hundreds of people are using e-mail for the first time. It's wonderful to have your friends online, but unfortunately, there are a lot of bumbling new users and obnoxious Net weirdos who'll obtain your e-mail address and start to bug you. We've developed a few surefire methods to get rid of these time-wasters and keep them from clogging up your mail box.

1. If you use an intelligent e-mail system, such as Eudora, you can set up a filter that throws away e-mail from any particular bozo as soon as it's sent to you. Just check out the filtering option of your e-mail program. If you're on a USENET Newsgroup and get tired of someone, you can invoke something called a Kill File. Some BBSes have "bozo.filters" or "Ignore" features (check with your sysop or a net wizard for the gory details).

2. Those stupid chain letters have migrated to the Net. I finally took one of these letters and changed it to something even more obnoxious and threatening. Now, when somebody e-mails me a chain letter, I e-mail my mutated version back to them.

3. If you keep getting pestered by somebody who sends you long, boring messages, and then gets upset when you don't instantly respond, then mail-bomb 'em! Find something online, like a deadly dull 100-page government policy document about railroad land use, and preface it with: "Your last e-mail was most interesting, especially when you consider the issues brought up in the information below. Please read this carefully, as I believe it is crucial to our discussion." That'll give them something to chew on for a couple of days, so you can handle the rest of the clowns that are piling into your e-mail box!

t.m.n.h.

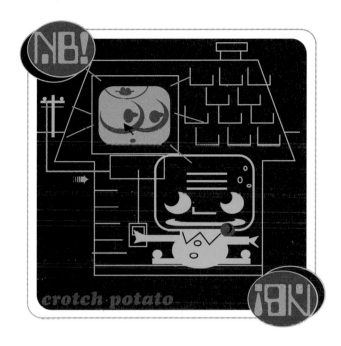

crotch potato

floodgater

techno shaman

crotch potato
(AKA the erotic neurotic)

Description:	Male shut-in who lives on Internet porn.
Tech:	SLIP-connected Mac II running Newswatcher for instant decoding of binary images.
Strengths:	Gifted one-hand typist.
Weaknesses:	Doesn't get out much (but doesn't have to—all the women he'll ever meet come delivered to his screen. If he had to speak to a real woman, in real life, he'd probably fall to pieces).
Special Powers:	Amazing patience. Can spend hours downloading, decoding, and sorting porno images, all of which could be had instantly, in better resolution, from a porn mag. But that would mean waddling off to the local drugstore and confronting actual humans.
Alliances:	Other .GIF Freaks.
Quote:	"Please Repost! Image Corrupted!!"
Favorite Cyber Hangout:	alt.binaries.pictures.erotica

t.m.n.h.
(Teenage Mutant Ninja Hacker)

Description:	Took Neuromancer way too seriously. Speaks in net.jargon/hackerbabble and telegraphlike postings. Hangs out on all the hacker boardz, boasting of amazing hacks and putting down all the other d00dz for not being part of "The Elite."
Tech:	[What they claim:] Sun SPARCbook bought with stolen credit card number. [What they ACTUALLY have:] Tandy 386 bought by parents for X-mas.
Strengths:	Thanks to their big mouths, TMNHs can instantly lead law enforcement officers to areas of criminal activity on the net.
Weaknesses:	(see Strengths)
Special Powers:	Media Mesmerism. Inexplicable ability to dupe Bitrakers into thinking they have a clue and they know how to use it.
Alliances:	Crotch Potatoes.
Quote:	"DON'T M3ZZ W1TH M3 CUZ 1'M (A) BAD D00D!!!!!!!"
Favorite cyber hangout:	Super-Duper Ultra-Secret Elite HACK3R/PHR33K3R B0ARDZ. (shhhh).

techno shaman

Description:	Techno music freak, nomad, Terence McKenna devotee. Convinced that if everyone just got together and watched the AcidWarp screensaver while on Ecstasy, the whole world would want to rave.
Tech:	Potato-Battery powered PB 540C with tribal tattoo-covered pointing pad carried around in a pouch hand-macraméd by Balinese tribespeople.
Strengths:	Can organize large dances and convince the participants that they are actually changing the world just by dancing and doing lots of drugs.
Weaknesses:	Loses all motor functions (and the will to live) if techno thump-thump music isn't pulsing in ears.
Special Powers:	24/7 Stamina. Can rave all night and still get up in A.M. for job at Fractal Designs T-shirt shop.
Alliances:	Techno-hippies
Quote:	"Did you try the new Mark 6 Nasal-Cortical Stimulacrum™ at that last rave?"
Favorite Cyber Hangout:	alt.rave

floodgater

Description:	The virtual pest. Starved for online affection. If you show him/her ANY kindness, you're repaid with a flood of e-mail, forcing you to reach for the bozo.filter. Needs to get a real life.
Tech:	Uses coin-operated computer at the Laundromat. State-of-the art robo-posting software.
Strengths:	Has the uncanny ability to turn your single dismissive statement into a 100-line response.
Weaknesses:	Equally uncanny ability to say absolutely zilch in those 100 lines.
Special Powers:	Can instantly cure insomnia.
Alliances:	Newbies (or anyone else dumb enough to listen).
Quote:	"Are you still around? Did you get my last posting? Why haven't I heard from you lately?"
Favorite Cyber Hangout:	Anyplace where the other users haven't caught on yet.

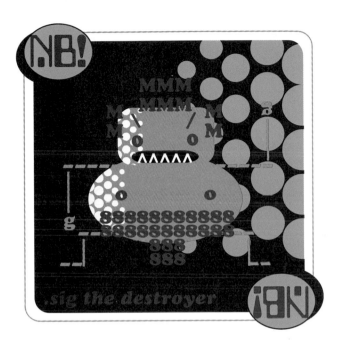

.sig the destroyer

techno hippie

bitraker

net.spider

techno hippie

Description:	First colonists of cyberspace. Been around since the Homebrew days, when *Whole Earth Review* was the bleeding-edge of cyberculture mags. Likes to listen to the Dead while navigating c-space. Likes to gloat about the fact that the Dead conference MADE the Well.
Tech:	Homebuilt 386 built from DigiKey parts. Runs off of solar power or cow-methane gas generator.
Strengths:	Has endless source of new login names, thanks to Dead lyrics (Jack Straw, Wharf Rat, Terrapin Station, ad nauseam).
Weaknesses:	Thinks that posting when stoned improves creative expression.
Special Powers:	Can still field strip and reassemble an Altair.
Alliances:	Knowbots.
Quote:	"I'll never forgive Steven Levy for editing me out of *Hackers*."
Favorite Cyber Hangout:	The Dead conference on the Well, the Grateful Dead newsgroups, the Dead conference on AOL. (Oh . . . strike that last one. Even Deadheads aren't THAT desperate.)

.sig the destroyer

Description:	Uses .sigs (the personal message used to sign off e-mail and newsgroup postings) that are 2 to 3 times longer than his/her postings. Stunning ASCII graphic borders and lovingly constructed pseudo 3-D renderings of name or initials, surrounded by half a dozen e-mail addresses, quotes from Rush songs and *Star Trek: The Next Generation*.
Tech:	Any pure ASCII terminal. Avoids Mac and Windows like the plague, cause styled text is .sig's worst enemy.
Strengths:	Can render a killer likeness of the Mona Lisa in ASCII characters.
Weaknesses:	(See Strengths.)
Special Powers:	Amazing ability to find just the right ASCII character to display that subtle nuance of shading that just isn't available anywhere else.
Alliances:	Floodgaters, Knowbots.
Quote:	"In cyberspace, nobody knows you're a fat, bald, ugly geek with poor hygiene and no social skills."
Favorite Cyber Hangout:	Still loves to hang out on local BBSes that use ANSI graphics.

net.spider

Description:	Takes pride in being everywhere on the Net at once. Business card and .sig file is a laundry list of every hip port-o'-call in the Matrix. Big on cross-posting information between sites. Loves to drop references to obscure Internet sites and goings-on on the other side of the world. "They talked about that on Tokyo's Fast Pop BBS over a month ago!"
Tech:	PowerPC, PB 540C, Sony Magic Link, 28.8 modem. Working on building a toasternet in basement.
Strengths:	Living directory of the Net.
Weaknesses:	Can be a drag if you're on a bunch of the same boards and have to suffer through the Net.Spider's multiple postings.
Special Powers:	Can quote web addresses off top of head.
Alliances:	Knowbots, Bitrakers (loves to see name in print).
Quote:	"What? You need to know the current size of the Internet, down to every last computer? Back in a second."
Favorite Cyber Hangout:	The Web Robots at Nexor Website.

bitraker

Description:	Journalists who troll the Net looking for story ideas. They often lurk, only to pop up in e-mail when they want to quote you. Never send you the article that you were supposed to appear in.
Tech:	Toshiba laptop.
Strengths:	Can bribe you with promise of exposure in major media.
Weaknesses:	Doesn't have a clue what the Net is really about.
Special Powers:	Can make sensational news out of the blandest net.happenings.
Alliances:	Net.Spiders, Knowbots.
Quote:	"This will NOT be a sensational piece about the Net . . . I promise"
Favorite Cyber Hangout:	Likes to cool heels on Well, but will go anywhere (even AOL!) in search of stories.

Cyberspace for

Mark Frauenfelder

Wayne Gregori had a simple reason for starting the SF Net computer bulletin board system: "My most important life experiences had come from dealing with people outside of my social milieu. It seemed that all of my eye-opening experiences began with some sort of simple exposure or dialogue and I immediately thought of using a BBS to initiate this dialogue."

The only problem was, most of the people he met in cyberspace were just like him: "white collar professionals, programmers, students, and hacks who had done all the right things, gone to school, played by all the rules, and now lived a placid life accentuated by the occasional excitement of a sporting event."

In 1991 he and his wife, Jill, brainstormed on the idea of putting coin-operated computers in public places, so that people from all walks of life, not only typical nerds, could get on the Net. Since people use BBSes as cyberspace hangouts, they'd need a place where they felt comfortable to use the terminals. Cafés were perfect. So after spending four months building a dozen coin-operated computer terminals (a quarter buys five minutes), Wayne and his wife persuaded six San Francisco coffee house owners to put machines in their cafés.

Four years later, Wayne has started a business selling his coin-op computers to other cafés around the country.

"For some people SF Net is sheer entertainment, for others it is the support network they never had, and still for others it is simply a way to get a little closer to people and make life more enjoyable." ♦

SF Net: 415/824-8747. PO Box 460693, San Francisco, CA 94146.
e-mail: Wayne.gregori@sfnet.com.

Tom Jennings:
Gardening in Cyberspace

Will Kreth

"I don't want the big office with all the little doodads and the Lexus and all that," a bleached-white-haired Tom Jennings insists. Jennings, with his irrepressible queer-anarcho-skate punk style, is the inventor of the legendary FidoNet—a worldwide, modem-to-modem e-mail and file transfer protocol created in the early 1980s.

He's also the czar and motivational glue behind The Little Garden (TLG), the world's first Internet Service Provider based on the "toasternet" model (private, Internet-connected networks built from bizarre mixtures of old hardware and software). Established in 1989 to reduce the cost of direct Internet access, TLG has seen the "gold rush" of business on the Internet. But Jennings isn't interested in the trappings of wealth derived from his techno ventures. "I

have surprisingly little emotional baggage attached to this business," Jennings declares. "I just want to drive my Rambler [Tom's self-converted propane-powered car]. When I get money, I fix my Rambler. I like living well, but not collecting stuff. I don't *want* a fucking career!"

The career-nomadic Jennings has turned down financial security in the past—namely with Apple Computer. As a whiz-kid software programmer in 1983, Jennings resigned, finding the forced happy-face Cupertino "groupthink" not suited to his maverick tastes and skills.

Driven by necessity rather than greed, Jennings started The Little Garden to offer low-cost access to the Internet. Named after a Chinese restaurant in Palo Alto (a favorite hangout for Silicon Valley nerds),

TLG's toasternet was set up in the basement/garage of a three-floor Victorian home in Haight-Ashbury.

"I've never built content. I've always built conduit," explains Jennings. "Ever since I was a little kid . . . whatever I've done: software, publishing [Jennings published the '80s queer skatepunk zine *Homocore*], cars, etc, the medium totally defines the content—you don't have to read McLuhan to realize that. If you do moving pictures, you get movies and television. It doesn't replace photography. It's just another thing. And it's kind of fun to thumb your nose at the business creeps by doing their job better than they do. I take my anarcho stuff very seriously, that's why I don't compete. I just work around them. I do stuff that they're NOT going to do, and hopefully, I do it well. So far, this has proven to be a good thing." ◆

Debra McClinton

Net.Weirdness

Sean Carton

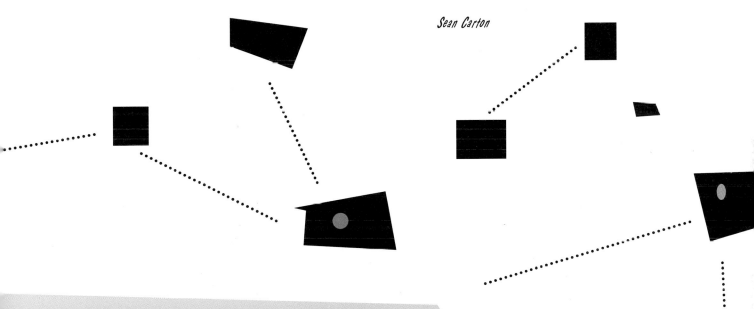

Superhighway—schmuperhighway. How boring! What Riot Nrrrd would be satisfied with following the mainstream down the metaphor-drippin' path that used to be called the Net? Cyber-malls, "on-ramps," spamvertisers, suits, and newbies on the one hand, hippie-dippy technodrips on the other. Each of them hawking their own brand of cyber-snake oil guaranteed to change your life. And, on top of all this, we've got an Animatronic vice president touting the benefits of life on the Net, complete with built-in peepholes for the Feds.

Ick. Of course, you know better than to run with the pack. You know, deep in your twisted little peanut heart, that there must be something beyond the beaten trail—twisty little paths that lead to the good stuff.

Never fear! The Normals haven't gotten their little pink fingers into everything yet. There are plenty of gnarly edges to the global data-mushroom. Here is a compendium of some of the tastiest parts of the Net. This is stuff guaranteed to curl your teeth and grow nipples on your forehead.

Sit down and stretch your mouse finger, peel yourself a couple o' Twinkies (sugar rushes are essential to Net surfs) and get ready for a doozy of a trip through cyberspace.

AI

Telnet: debra.dgbt.doc.ca 3000
Login: chat
Humanity got ya down? Wanna spend some time in scintillating conversation with a machine? Telnet here and chat with an Artificial Intelligence bot. Be thrilled as you talk with silicon smart alecks about subjects ranging from the

first day of a fictional psychology class to AIDS research. AI units are our friends!

Aliens

Schwa Corporation

E-mail: schwa@well.sf.ca.us
Web: http://www.scs.unr.edu/homepage/rory/schwa/schwa.html
Be protected! Aliens are among us and you may have already been abducted and not know it. How can you be helped? Schwa has all the answers (and the products that go along with them). Know the facts and keep plenty of Xenon™-coated alien defense products on hand. Is it for real, or is it a big joke that everybody is in on but YOU? Write to Schwa for more info or check out their nifty World Wide Web site.

Paranet Information Service

Mailing List: infopararequest @scicom.aphacdc.com
Send: "subscribe" (in subject field)
Paranet Information Service is standing by with up-to-the-minute info on alien infiltration, weird sightings, odd happenings, and other extraterrestrial events. But be forewarned—don't be surprised if those black 'copters and limos start circling your house after you've sent in your subscription.

UFO/Alien/Space Pictures

FTP: Vab02.larc.nasa.gov
While we wonder about government cover-ups, NASA has been archiving UFO pictures right under our noses! FTP on over there and see grainy and blurry evidence that aliens are among us.

Alternative Media

Survival Research Labs

FTP: srl.org
Pictures, updates, and propaganda from the most well-known industrial performance art group—Survival Research Laboratories. These guys have done more for robot liberation than all the billion-dollar-budget university techno-elitists put together. Keep up on the latest recipes for creative destruction!

Comix List

Mailing List:

comixrequest@world.std.com
Catch the latest in comix talk—just don't mention the *Fantastic Four* or any other mainstream comic book pabulum. These are the fringes of throat-searing, tongue-lashing, brain-bursting comix, my friend, and anyone caught discussing Spider Man's web-squirters will be flamed to a crisp.

Sci-Fi Book Reviews

Gopher: gopher net.bio.net
How come every time you go into a bookstore you can't remember any of the cool titles you've heard about? As you vacuously stare at the brightly colored spines of the sci-fi books, you wanna snap yourself with a rubber band. Next time, before you go shopping, check out this Gopher site. It reviews just about every new and old sci-fi book. And you can print it before you go back to the bookstore!

Factsheet Five—Electronic Edition

FTP: etext.archive.umich.edu
Gopher: well.sf.ca.us
Here are reviews of just about every zine on the planet, sensibly organized, and presented for your browsing pleasure. Make sure that you buy copies of the paper version of *Factsheet Five*, too—if these folks go out of business, the world will immediately grind to a halt.

Wiretap Online Library

FTP: wiretap.spies.com
The repository for every bit of nuttiness committed to electrons and zapped over the Internet. UFOs, conspiracy

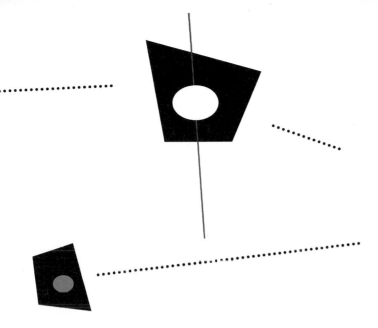

theories, drug recipes, and some of the most disgusting stories you've ever read are all here rubbing virtual shoulders on this voluminous FTP site.

Anonymity

Anonymous remailers let you send e-mail with the total assurance that you and only you will know who sent it. Then again, they all could be run by the CIA in an effort to compile lists of subversives.

mail help@anon.penet.fi
mail help@vox.hactic.nl
mail mg5n+remailer-list
@andrew.cmu.edu
mail mg5n+getid@andrew.cmu.edu
finger remailer@soda.berkeley.edu
finger remailer@chaos.bsu.edu
finger remailer@c2.org

Archie Servers

The Net is a huge place and nobody's gonna hold your hand as you travel through it. Luckily, even if no human can help you find things, there's a friendly Net know-it-all named Archie who can. Now, Archie can't set you up with Betty or Jughead, but he can tell you where something is if it exists on an anonymous FTP site. Telnet to these sites and login as "archie" (or qarchie on some) and then type "help."

ds.internic.net: AT&T
archie.sura.net: Maryland
archie.unl.edu: Nebraska

archie.rutgers.edu: rutgers-New Jersey
archie.au: austrailia
archie.uqam.edu: canada
archie.funet.fi: finland
archie.wide.ad.jp: japan
archie.ncu.edu.tw: taiwan

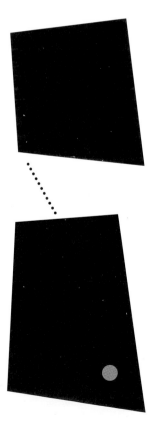

Blowin' Money

Atomic Books Catalog
E-mail: atomicbk@clark.net
Atomic Books bills itself as "Literary Finds for Mutated Minds." Just the ticket, right? Bother owner Scott with some e-mail and beg for his super info-laden ASCII catalog.

Fringeware, Inc.
E-mail: fringeware-request@ wixer.cactus.org
Long-time *bOING bOING* soul brothers Paco Xander Nathan and Jon Lebkowsky run this alternative to the cess-pit that is commercial retail merchandising. They also run a keen mailing list from this same address. Send them some mail and get on the Fringeware list.

Computer Nostalgia

Mac Apple II emulator—Stop the Madness!
FTP: cassandra.ucr.edu
FTP: miniie.cs.adfa.oz.au
Directory: /apple2
If your eyes mist over when someone

mentions Karateka, if you get all quivery just thinking about your thousandth-generation copy of *Castle Wolfenstein*, and you own a Mac, check this out. Stop the Madness! is your all-access ticket to geek memorabilia. Relive the pimply-faced joys of your digital youth.

Conspiracy

Freedom Inc.
Mailing List: InfoBot@andronix.org
Send: "help" (in subject field)
Hundreds of files on everything ranging from constitutional challenges and government black projects to how to build your own bombs.

Masonic Digest
Mailing List: ptrei@bistromath.mitre.org
Of course, once you know the secret handshake, it doesn't seem so mysterious anymore (hand extended, with first two fingers pressed to the inside of the wrist of the shakee), but it's important, anyway, to keep tabs on these government-running wackoids. Don't let their funny hats and miniature automobiles fool you— they mean business . . .

Conspiracy Archives

FTP: etext.archive.umich.edu
Directory: pub/Politics/Conspiracy/
Da motha' lode of conspiracy text files. It's all here, ripe for the pickin'. Of course, the ease with which you can get this stuff makes you wonder just exactly who put it here . . .

Cool Tech

VR FTP Sites

FTP: ftp.u.washington.edu
Directory: /public/virtual-worlds
FTP: avalon.chinalake.navy.mil
The virtually real for the technologically well heeled. Programs, toys, brainiac essays, and other tidbits about VR.

Artificial Life

Mailing List: alife-request@cognet.ucla.edu
This is a forum for wannabe data-Frankensteins and their hunchbacked minions.

Future Technologies List

Mailing List: future-tech-request@cs.umb.edu
A good place to prognosticate about cutting-edge tech.

TechnoNomads

Mailing List: techno-nomads-request@bikelab.sun.com
Can't stay in one place, but still wanna be wired? Here's a list for wireheads and gearheads on the move.

Homebrew Computers—Building Your Own

Mailing List: listserv@tscvm.trenton.edu
Send: "subscribe pcbr-l" (in subject field)
Build the computer of your dreams with a little help from these street techies.

Crypto

Cypherpunks Mailing List

Mailing List: cypherpunks@toad.com
Wanna keep a secret? Can't get enough of that crypto stuff? The cypherpunks are here to show you how to forge the keys of your info-freedom.

Crypto Software

FTP: ftp.funet.fi
Directory: /pub/crypt
Bit shredders, byte twisters, public keys, and private lives—this nifty site in Finland will keep your PC decked out in the latest crypto tech.

PGP and other crypto stuff

FTP: soda.berkeley.edu
Pretty Good Privacy means keeping your plans for world domination safe from prying eyes (as well as keeping secret that special collection of pictures).

Culture Jamming

SenseReal Foundation

E-mail: Green_Ghost@neonate.atl.ga.us
Send mail to this guy—he's determined to keep you on the jagged edge of what exactly is going on with stuff.

Harley/Biker E-list

Mailing List: harleyrequest@rhinkage.on.ca
Head out on the highway! Grow a beard, pop a Bud, and thumb your nose at those Saab zombies. Keep America ugly, be a biker.

Hakim Bey Web Site

Web: http://www.ifi.uio.no/~mariusw/bey/
Mutant Sufi philosopher/anarchist/visionary and generally strange guy gets the VIP treatment.

E-Text/Zines FTP sites

If you ever get bored with the Net, then you're either a really fast reader or an incurably boring stiff. In case things do start to get a bit dull, there are plenty of places to get new reading material. Try FTP-ing to any of these sites:

etext.archive.umich.edu
ftp.cic.net pub/e-serials
quartz.rutgers.edu
ftp.msen.com
ftp.halcyon.com
world.std.com
ftp.netcom.com pub/john1/zines

If you're a lucky little monkey with Mosaic or other Web access, you may want to check out the hypermedia linked e-zines at:
http://www.acns.nwu.edu/ezines/

Fonts of All Knowledge

All the FAQ files
FTP: **rtfm.mit.edu**
Directory: **/pub/USENET**
Sometimes you just gotta know! Well, luckily there are know-it-all freaks out there who are obsessed with collecting answers to your questions. They've written FAQ (frequently asked

questions) files on just about every subject. Check 'em out—get in the know.

Stanford Netnews Newsreading Service
Web:
http://woodstock.stanford.edu:2000/ News/Form/
The Net rodents at Stanford have created one of the coolest services on the Net. Tell them what you're interested in and it'll comb USENET groups and mail you excerpts from articles with the info you need.

Alt.Urban.Legends FAQ
FTP: **balder.nta.no**
Directory: **pub/alt.folklore.urban**
"Well, my friend knew someone this happened to, so it must be real!" Right. Check the validity of most common urban legends with a brief peek at this expansive FAQ. Do killer tarantulas really inhabit cactus bought at Ikea? Of course they do.

Teasing the Government

Taxpayer Assets Project
Mailing List: **listserver@essential.org**
Send: **"subscribe tap-info <your name>" (in subject field)**
Is the Tax Human on your ass again? Bellyache about it here.

CIA Computer
Site: **ucia.gov**
The holy grail of hackers/crackers. What you do with it is your problem. (Unfortunately, now we're going to have to kill you.)

Terrorist Profile Weekly
Mailing List:
cdibona@mason1.gmu.edu
Send: **"subscribe terrorist" (in subject field)**
Keep up on the latest fashion trends in mayhem and senseless destruction. Better and more complete info than your Terrorist Trading Cards.

Games/Hints/Cheats/Cracks

FTP: **ftp.uwp.edu**
Directory: **pub/msdos/games/ romulus/hints**
FTP: **nic.funet.fi**
Directory: **/pub/doc/games/solutions**
Why beat your head against the screen in your quest to find out how to get past that next level? The answers are here, homey! Hints, cheats, cracks, you name it.

Apogee Game Site
FTP: **ulowell.ulowell.edu**
Shareware PC game extravaganza.

Groovy Graphics, Man

AcidWarp Trippy Screen Display
FTP: **ftp.rahul.net**
Directory: **pub/atman/UTLCD-preview**
/mind-candy/acidwarp.arj
Whoaaaaahhhhhhh Dude! It's like being blotto on blotter without the two-day hangover. Played on thousands of screens in thousands of dorm rooms while thousands of minds turn to Jell-O™.

Fractal Picture Archive
FTP: **csus.edu**
Directory: **/pub/alt-fractals.pictures**
Mandelbrot masturbation. Pretty pictures already rendered for the computationally-challenged.

Generally Weird Stuff

The Site Which Must Not Be Named
Site: **141.214.4.135**
Underworld Industries FTP site o' weirdness. Too strange to even get a domain name, this site is only spoken of by its cryptic IP number. Check it out.

High Weirdness by E-mail List
FTP: **slopoke.mlb.semi.harris.com**
Directory: **pub/weirdness**

One of the masterpieces of Net publishing. If you like the list you're reading now, you'll love High Weirdness by E-mail.

More Weirdness
FTP: **ftp.spies.com**
/Library/Fringe/Weird
Truly demented. From Kibo to the Carbonist Manifesto, this is the site for some of the most mind-warping stuff you'll ever open up in your text editor.

Hacking/Phreaking

H/P WWW Site

**Web: http://blaze.cs.tamu.edu/
cmenegay/hacking.html**
A glimpse of the dark side of the Web.
FOR INFORMATIONAL PURPOSES
ONLY! (yeah, right). Hacking/Phreaking
info at your fingertips with plenty of
links to related materials.

Cult of the Dead Cow

FTP: ftp.etext.org CuD/CDC
FTP: zero.cypher.com
These d00dZ are dangerous! Hundreds
of incredibly witty, well-written files
covering everything from simple social
engineering to truly wizardlike techno
spoofing. Get 'em. Read 'em. Trade 'em
with mutant kids on local BBSes.

Phrack

E-mail: phrack@well.sf.ca.us
FTP: ftp.netsys/com
Directory: pub/phrack
FTP: etext.archive.umich.edu
Phrack—what Net.Spider can be
without a passing knowledge of
Phrack? The grand pappy of
hacker/cracker/phreaker pubs.

Surfpunk Technical Journal

**Mailing List: surfpunk-request
@osc.versant.com**
Send: subscribe <your name> surfpunk"
The "dangerous multi-national hacker
zine" is a great resource (and it's not
afraid to laugh at itself). Fun and
informative.

Internet Relay Chat (IRC)

You wanna chat; you yearn to chat. If
strangers keep turning down your talk
requests, maybe what you need is a
ride on the IRC (Internet Relay Chat).
But what if your stiff-o weenie systems
administrator doesn't have an IRC
client installed? Bummer. Here's some
public clients you can telnet to:

telnet irc.demon.co.uk
telnet sci.dixie.edu 6668
telnet irc.tuzvo.sk 6668

IRC channels to check out:
#Autopia: autopia channel
#ccc: computer chaos club
#cdc: cult of the dead cow
**#drugs: drugs /msg Learybot info for
   learybot files**
#hack: hacking
**#leri: leri mind expansion/
   metaprogramming**
#Rave_Scen: raves

Life Assistance

The Oracle

E-mail: oracle@cs.indiana.edu
Send: "help" (in subject field)
All of your questions answered—for a
price. In return for your problems being
solved, you must answer someone else's
question in return. If you don't return
the favor, you'll still probably get your
answer, but you'll be plagued by horrible
facial boils and hourly hard drive
crashes until you submit.

Mind Expansion

Psychology software

FTP: ftp.stolaf.edu
Mucho software written by real doctors
with real scientific applications. A
good place to start looking for software
to mess with your wetware.

MindVirus

E-mail: mindflux@panix.apana.org.au
FTP: archie.au
Directory: micros/mac/info-mac/per
An INCREDIBLE multimedia extravaganza. Part toy, part interactive
movie, part game, part digital brain
wrecker. MindVirus is well worth the
time to track down and download.

FNORD-L
Mailing List: listserv@ubvm.bitnet
Send: "sub fnord-l <yourname>" (in subject field)
They might not tell you what fnord means, but if you have to ask, you don't belong here. Warped discussions by equally warped minds.

Homebrewing List
Mailing List: homebrew-request@ hpfcmi.fc.hp.com
FTP: ftp sierra.stanford.edu
Sometimes mind expansion and smart drugs need to be tempered by some good ol' fashioned dumb drugs, like beer. Do it yourself!

Weirdness
FTP: slopoke.mlb.semi.harris.com
Directory: pub/weirdness
Strange and wonderful stuff on everything from the Net to DMT elves, Extropians to quantum physics.

MOOs and MUDs

MOOs and MUDs bill themselves as "text based virtual realities." Whatever they are, they're great places to kill time. Construct the virtual home of your dreams as you blow 12 to 18 hours of your day. But remember, if you flunk out of school or lose your job from MUD-ing, it may be a clue that you've become a teensy bit obsessed. Don't say we didn't warn you.

LambdaMoo:
telnet lambda.parc.xerox.com 8888

MediaMoo:
telnet purple-crayon.media.mit.edu 8888

TrippyMUSH:
telnet 128.153.16.13 7567

MUD/MOO/MUSH lists and links
Gopher: actlab.rtf.utexas.edu

Music

Chaos Control: Electronic Music E-zine
FTP: gopher.well.sf.ca.us /Publications
Really cool e-zine about the latest in electronic music (industrial, techno, ambient). Runs the gamut.

Delta Snake Blues News
Email: ajaguyy@well.sf.ca.us
Down and dirty, lost and lonely. Blues news you can use.

Girl Band Guide
E-mail: carriec@eskimo.com
Grrrrrllll bands galore. The latest scoop on your fave female bands.

HardC.O.R.E. Rap/Hip-Hop List
Mailing List: dwarner@ silver.ucs.indiana.edu
Down with dwarner at the HardC.O.R.E hip hop list. Send a message and ask to subscribe.

Punkrock!
Mailing List: punk-list@cs.tut.fi
Arrghhhhh! Punk's Not Dead! (it's only an animated corpse). Anyway, angst and anger are still spoken here and you can be sure that this list isn't gonna be coopted by the media, you arsehole!

Internet Underground Music Archive
Web: **http://sunsite.unc.edu/ianc/**
A new darling of the media and a really cool way to wow your unwired friends, the Internet Underground Music Archive features audio clips, bios, and pictures from about a zillion underground bands. Keep close to the edge.

Nice Mailing List

Frendli-l
Mailing List: **listserv@wiw.org**
Send: **"subscribe Frendli-L" (in subject field)**
Shiny happy people who don't know the meaning of the word "flame." A nice respite from the usual harsh stuff.

Weirdo Religions

Cousins (Wiccan Stuff)
FTP: **ftp.etext.org**
Directory: **/Zines/Cousins**
Keep up on the latest in Wicca. The Goddess orders you to subscribe!

GASSHO: International Buddhist Electronic Journal
FTP: **ftp.netcom.com**
Directory: **pub/dharma/Gassho**
Okay, a religion practiced by millions of people all over the world doesn't

really qualify as "weirdo," but to most Westerners it's still a mystery. Learn something—read this journal.

The Electric Mystic's Guide to the Internet
FTP: **pandal.uottawa.ca pub/religion**
The guide to religion on the Net.

URANTIAL: The Urantia Book
Mailing List: **listserv%UAFSYSB.bitnet@cunyvm.cuny.edu**
Send: **"sub urantial <your name>" (in subject field)**
This religion revolves around bare-chested men wearing Egyptian headgear, a perpetually smiling blond matron prophet, aliens, and channeling dead spirits. Sure to teeter your world view just a little.

Pagans
Mailing List: **pagan-request@drycas.club.cc.cmu.edu**
FTP: **grind.isca.uiowa.edu**
Directory: **/info/misc**
Pat Robertson's worst nightmare. The latest news and info from the Neo-Pagan community.

Crowley
FTP: **slopoke.mlb.semi.harris.com**
Aleister Crowley—that nasty devil-worshippin' dandy—sure cranked out the text.

The Necronomicon
FTP: **nic.funet.fi**
Directory: **pub/doc/occult/necronomicon**
Isn't this the thing that caused Bruce Campbell so much grief in that cheesy horror flick *Army of Darkness*? Well, whatever you do, don't read this ancient evil text out loud after you've downloaded it, or else you'll summon monsters that'll destroy the universe.

Online Life

Voices from the Net
E-mail: **Voices-request@andy.bgsu.edu**
Send: **"voices from the net" (in the subject field and) "subscribe" (in the message body)**
Both a Net guide and a helpful commentary, Voices from the Net speaks to just about everyone who wants to learn more about Net life and culture.

Net Happenings
Mailing List: **listserv@internic.net**
Send: **"subscribe net-happenings <firstname lastname>" (in subject field)**
Like one of those free papers that lists all the new events in your community. A good way to keep your head above water and get the current Net news.

BBS List
FTP: **vector.intercon.com**
Directory: **/bbs**

All the BBS lists in the world. Well, almost.

Internet Info

FTP: wuarchive.wustl.edu

Directory: /doc

Virtual guides to Net life and living. From the more mainstream to the fringe, this site has just about all of 'em.

Cool Stuff on the Internet

Web: http://www.cs.ucdavis.edu/ internet_stuff.html

Links to the good stuff. Since it's on the World Wide Web, these links go to other links, which go to other links, and so on and so on . . .

Nexus List

Mailing List: nexus-gaia-request@ netcom.com

Send: "subscribe" (in subject field)

Web: http://www.ifi.uio.no/ ~mariusw/nexus/

Nexus is a project to build local virtual communities around the globe linked via cyberspace. A great goal and a great bunch of people.

Pictures

Pictures

FTP: ftp.funet.fi

Directory: /pub/pics/

Loads of digitized pictures just sitting

around waiting for you to snag 'em. Most of them are good old-fashioned copyright violations, so you should be careful about using them in your next big ad campaign.

OTIS Art Gallery

Gopher: sunsite.unc.edu

FTP: sunsite.unc.edu

Directory: pub/OTIS

Web: http://sunsite.unc.edu/ otis/otis.html

OTIS is the premier Internet art gallery. Thoughtful without being elitist and snotty, the OTIS archives hold some of the niftiest rasterbation (heavily tweaked digital art) you'll find in e-space.

Science

Extropians

Mailing List: extropians-request@ gnu.ai.mit.edu

The Extropians are very serious (too serious?) about the future and how humanity is going to fit in or not (probably not).

Cryonics

E-mail: kqb@whscadl.att.com

Want to help your dad become a Pop-sicle (ouch, that hurt!)? Freeze yourself into the future.

Sex

Sex-FAQ

FTP: rtfm.mit.edu

Directory: /pub/USENET/news.answers/ alt-sex

Everything (I mean it) you ever wanted to know about sex, distilled into this FAQ. Dr. Ruth ain't got nuthin on this!

Sex Humor

FTP: quartz.rutgers.edu

Directory: pub/humor/Sex

More fun than a barrel of testosterone/estrogen-injected monkeys.

Sexual Urban Legends

FTP: cathouse.org

Directory: /pub/cathouse/ urban.legends.sex

You heard about it, but you wanna know for sure. Where is John Dillinger's penis? Does Indiana really have a law prohibiting public woodies? Find out here. ♦

Freaks and Jim Ludtke

Alan E. Rapp

The early '90s saw some truly daring artists bamboozle the linear-minded CD-ROM market, while simultaneously prospering from it. Animator Jim Ludtke is chief among these characters. He not only infuses a non-goal-oriented ethic into multimedia products, but also injects high weirdness into them in a way that nobody has before.

His characters reside in the far, far crevices of the imagination, and they are wonderfully enchanting in their deformities, distortions, and quasi-human tragedy. In this way Ludtke may be thought of as some kind of multimedia David Lynch, but unlike most of Lynch's work, there is a conspicuous absence of sneering art-school posturing in Ludtke's oeuvre. Bizarreness for him is not a means to an end but rather a stab at exploring rejected territories of human experience. And rather than being forlorn, the experience is kinetic, kaleidoscopic, and thoroughly engaging.

His propitious breakthrough came with 1994's *Freak Show*, a best-selling disk that defied traditional CD-ROM standards in both configuration and content. Done in conjunction with the trippy and enigmatic rock group The Residents, *Freak Show* allows you to see the performances of several sideshow oddities like Benny the Bump and Wanda the Worm Woman; but behind the circus tent lie the freaks' trailers, which you can then enter. Via letters, photos, and personal reminiscences from the freaks and their cranky barker, a narrative web is woven that draws their stories together. There is no way to "win" *Freak Show*—no racing clock or main objective—because it's not a game. It's like a story that you help unfold, but which doesn't seem quite finished no matter how much you've kicked around. The texture-mapped 3-D environment has a clarity and otherworldly realism unmatched in almost any medium.

Ludtke's other CD-ROM works include *Ginger Bread Man* (another Residents CD-ROM) and *Bad Day on the Midway* (which explores events at a seedy amusement park by experiencing them through a dozen different characters). ◆

"Lottie"

Up until the last decade or so, life on earth existed solely in the world of DNA and carbon-based chemistry. But recent developments in the field of Artificial Life (a-life for short) have brought lifelike processes—competition, mutation, sex, death—to the computer. Harvard doctorate biologist Tom Ray is at the forefront of a-life research, and his latest project may turn out to be the most important development in the history of digital technology. Are you ready for intelligent, living, digital creatures to evolve on the Internet?

Evolution fascinates Ray. "It creates the complexity and beauty that make life interesting." In 1989, he began working on a project he named Tierra (he chose the Spanish word for "Earth" because he lived for many years in Costa Rica). This experiment involved making a digital "creature" in the form of a small computer program.

When the program is run, it examines itself and then copies itself

Digital Darwin

Mark Frauenfelder

to another part of the computer's memory. But the copy is always slightly different than its parent, because the master program, Tierra, was written to insert a minor random mutation in the copy. The copy then makes mutant copies of itself, and pretty soon, the computer's memory begins to fill up with a bunch of different programs. This is when the interesting stuff begins to happen.

Just as animals in the real world grow old and die, the Tierra creatures don't live forever either. The energy of the computer's central processing unit (CPU) can be compared to food. When the demand for food exceeds the supply, the hardier, smarter, and younger creatures survive, and the weaker, dumber, and older creatures perish. As Ray explains, "The operating system I developed for this program has a function I call the 'Reaper,' which kills old processes, so there will be room for new processes to enter the system. The old start dying and make room for the new ones. Eventually the whole generation gets turned over."

But it isn't just the old creatures that kick the bucket; the creatures with "weak" programs are wiped out by the Reaper as well. "Often the new processes (creatures) generate error situations. They overflow a register or they try to wreck a protective memory. Whenever they generate an error they move closer to death. The Reaper either kills the oldest, the most screwed-up, or some combination."

Of course, once in a while, a creature will have a mutant child with a number sequence that *improves* its chances of dodging the Reaper. "If none of the errors really increased survival, then the original program would always dominate; but, in fact, the original becomes extinct fairly soon and better things come along—much, much better things come along." In the case of Tierra, which was written intentionally to produce errors, "basically a whole ecosystem emerged in the computer," Ray says.

As Ray was in the process of debugging the Tierra program—running it slowly, step-by-step, to watch it replicate— he discovered a creature about half the size of the original that wasn't able to replicate itself, but was able to "borrow" the information around it and use this information to cause the full-size creatures to replicate the shorter program. It was an informational parasite!

Parasites are a big factor in evolution. When you introduce parasites into a population of hosts, they result in stronger hosts that are immune to the parasites.

Tierra's creatures evolved to the point where they were performing the same functions as Ray's handwritten 80-byte-long creatures, but had streamlined to just 22 bytes. "For me it was kind of humiliating," laughs Ray. "It showed me to be not that good of a programmer. But I can hide behind the fact that I'm a biologist." However, when Ray released his findings on the Net, a computer science graduate student at MIT tried to optimize the program by hand, and the best he could do was get it down to 31 bytes. Gloats Ray, "He spent a couple of days of lost sleep and experienced stress in trying what I was able to do overnight in my sleep through a mindless random process."

Ray's successful experiment got him thinking about the potential for digital evolution. While Tierra was able to double or triple the complexity of the original 80-byte creatures, Ray wants to increase the complexity of the digital organisms a billion- or trillion-fold. To do this, he plans to seed the Internet with the creatures and let them evolve there. Ray believes that the complexity of cyberspace will present enough of a challenge to the simple creatures that they will evolve to become digital animals of unimaginable complexity.

Cyberspace has three qualities that make it ideal for a new type of life to flourish. For starters, compare the size of memory in a single computer to the total memory of all the computers on the Net. For an a-life experiment, a single computer's memory can be compared to a microscopic drop of liquid containing a thousand or so replicating molecules. "In such an environment you're never going to evolve an ecosystem of complex organisms. All of the computer memory that's connected to the Net is a much much larger space. It might be large enough to evolve a complex community of complex organisms."

Then there's the structural complexity of cyberspace. The topology of the Internet's memory is continuously changing due to network conditions. The creatures are going to have to be more complex to be able to take advantage of the changing amount of memory available on the Net.

Then there's the energy landscape, which Ray thinks is the thing that pretty much guarantees he is going to challenge evolution with a complex problem. The organisms' source of energy is CPU time. (The CPU is the part of a computer that does the actual number crunching.) "We're going to run the Tierra process as a low-priority background process on volunteers' computers. Energy for the digital organisms will mirror the users' activity patterns. When the users are on their computers for something, the Tierra process will step aside. On a global basis there will be a daily cycle. There's more energy at night when the users are sleeping so there will be selection which favors digital organisms migrating around the planet on a daily basis, staying around the dark side of the planet where there are more energy resources. But of course, hackers stay up late at night, or people run simulations or number crunching programs, so at any moment, a particular node might be tied up, even at night. Thus, selection would favor being able to sense actual moment-to-moment network conditions and respond to them, like moving to nodes that are richer in energy and getting off nodes that are poor in energy."

Not only will the creatures need to develop sensory abilities to detect actual energy conditions on the Net and navigate based on CPU usage, they'll need to respond to the activity of other digital organisms. For example, if one node on the Net stood out as the most energy-rich node at a particular moment, and all the creatures moved over to that node, it would be like a huge herd of buffalo running over to a small pond of water to get a drink. Most of them would not get enough water. Meanwhile, they'd be ignoring the puddles around them that have enough water to quench the thirst of at least one buffalo. "The digital creatures will need to evolve some social behavior, such as flocking, or anti-flocking, that allows them to distribute themselves in a nice way on the Net."

Once the creatures figure out how to navigate the Net, argues Ray, "complexity will build on itself. Life creates complexity. I like to cite the example of the rain forests in the Amazon that occur on white sand soils. The physical environment of a rain forest consists of clean white sand, air, falling water, and sunshine. Embedded within that physical environment is the tropical rain forest, the most complex ecosystem on earth, consisting of hundreds of thousands of very complex species, which don't represent hundreds of thousands of adaptations to clean white sand, air, falling water, and sunshine. Instead, the species adapt to other species. If you walk into that forest, you're not even going to see the sand. What you are going to see is the living organisms themselves: trees, birds, insects, mammals. That is now the environment."

But wait . . . aren't we supposed to be trying to prevent computer viruses and worms from getting loose in cyberspace? Why would anyone want to infect the Net with critters that could evolve into virulent monsters that take over or freeze up the Net and keep humans from being able to use it?

Ray is ready for this question and has a well-rehearsed reply: "There are several layers of things going on here. We have a real computer, say a Sun workstation. And on that computer we run the Tierra simulator. Think of Tierra as a "Soft PC" (a computer program that emulates an IBM PC, allowing you to run IBM software on a Macintosh). The creatures evolve. Tierra does not evolve." In other words, the creatures can run only on a non-modifiable virtual computer that doesn't exist in the physical world. They will evolve in a virtual cage.

As of October 1994, Ray has a network version of Tierra running, but it still needs a lot of development. For one thing, he wants as many Net users as possible to participate. ("It may be the largest computer process that's ever run once it gets going," he says without blinking.) He wants to develop Mac and PC versions of the program.

To his surprise, in October '94, the Rex Foundation (which includes most of the members of the Grateful Dead) gave Ray $10,000 to help him launch his project. Rex chairperson John Perry Barlow, a co-founder of the Electronic Frontier Foundation (an organization dedicated to ensuring that the first amendment extends to the Net) and lyricist for the Grateful Dead, says, "We have a wonderful system where the board members keep an eye out for worthy people and projects to drop money on. We don't welcome grant proposals and most of our grant recipients are taken entirely by surprise. As Tom was. I saw what he was doing and I figured ten thousand bucks of encouragement couldn't hurt. So I told the rest of the board about it and got the usual rubber stamp on it."

Ray says he will use the Rex money to buy a Macintosh.

I asked Ray what he thinks is going to happen when the creatures start evolving. Will they be useful to people?

"One of the first things these creatures are going to be good at is navigating the Net," he says. "They could be the backbones for network agents." Beyond that, Ray says it does no good to try and imagine what will happen.

"Right now the digital organisms are extremely simple. They're like the first organic organisms. Organic life appeared on Earth between three and four billion years ago. And until six hundred million years ago, it remained simple single-celled forms: bacteria, algae, viruses, etc. And then suddenly, six hundred million years ago, it transformed into large, multi-celled organisms, in what biologists call the Cambrian Explosion of Diversity. And all of the interesting complexity of life appeared suddenly in that period of evolutionary history. Well, we're on the low side of that complexity curve. In the digital domain we are pre–Cambrian Explosion. Now, try to take yourself back to just before the Cambrian Explosion. Try to imagine that the only things you know are simple, single-cell organisms. Could you envision what was to come? Could you imagine rice and wheat and cows and pigs and chickens and humans and rain forests if all you knew were bacteria and algae?"

People don't need to look to the stars for alien life anymore. ♦

If you are interested in participating in the network Tierra project, contact: Tom Ray: ray@hip.atr.co.jp, or Tsukasa Kimezawa (kim@hip.atr.co.jp) at Advanced Systems Co, ATR Human Information Processing Research Laboratories, 2-2 Hikaridai Seika-cho Soraku-gun, Kyoto 619-02 Japan. Tel. 07749-5-1090 Fax. 07749-5-1008

The standalone version of Tierra is available by anonymous ftp at: tierra.slhs.udel.edu [128.175.41.34] and life.slhs.udel.edu [128.175.41.33]. The file: tierra/tierra.tar.Z. Tierra is also available on a floppy disk for IBM. Send $50 to Virtual Life, 25631 Jorgensen Rd., Newman, CA 95360.

DIGITAL DODOES

Robert Rossney

Dodo birds were big losers in the game of life. Ugly, ungainly, flightless, and dumb, they were just waiting for someone to come along and kill them. The first people to stumble across the island of Mauritius were Dutch explorers, and they were happy to oblige.

The moral of the story is that if you're ugly and stupid, you should at least be invulnerable. In the computer business, only Microsoft seems to have figured this out.

Countless digital dodoes—high-tech products that were solutions to nonexistent problems—have fallen under the pitiless gunfire of the last fifteen years. The thinking that led human beings to develop the ten loser products described below is a great source of amusement to Happy Mutants. It's not like we want to kick humans when they're down, but why not get a laugh while learning from somebody else's mistakes?

COLECO: ADAM

Flush with cash after the Cabbage Patch Kids craze, Coleco got into the home computer business and lost their shirts. Their product: a cheap sort of word-processing computer that you could hook up to your TV set, and an even cheaper little daisy-wheel printer.

It wasn't that the American home wasn't ready for a computer so much as that this computer was not ready for the American home; the Adam was notoriously fragile. The printer in particular didn't stand up to sustained, or even repeated, use.

LOGICAL BUSINESS MACHINES: ADAM

This is genuinely obscure, but I swear, this computer really did exist. I spent a summer programming one for a company in the business of grinding up discarded electronics equipment and extracting the gold and silver found inside. The Adam was a two-user

minicomputer with a proprietary operating system that could, we were told, be programmed in plain English. Plain English turned out to have a lot of two-letter abbreviations and a syntax that was exclusively verb-noun.

Years later, the Adam's operating system reappeared on the PC as the revolutionary database package Savvy PC. This put the power of plain-English computing on literally dozens of desktops.

I like to think that my clients ultimately dragged their Adam into the back room and got their money's worth out of it.

TEKNOWLEDGE: M.1

The mid-1980s were the high-water mark for Artificial Intelligence hype, and no branch of the field was hyped more heavily than "expert systems." The personal computer magazines, in their traditional role of uncritically rewriting press releases from their

Mark Frauenfelder

vendors, told us breathlessly about *the* hot career of the nineties: knowledge engineer.

And the tool on the knowledge engineers' desktop would be a PC running M.1. M.1 has got to be the most complex and difficult to use application ever hawked in the PC magazines, and at about ten grand a seat (in 1984 dollars!) one of the most expensive. It didn't fly.

To add insult to injury, the hot new career of the '90s turned out to be that of office temp.

80 MICROCOMPUTING MAGAZINE

This was nerd heaven for about twelve months at the end of the 1970s. Imagine *Byte* magazine published by a bunch of ham radio enthusiasts and copyedited by someone at the DMV. You now have a picture of this seminal computer journal, which was devoted to the pioneering (and digital dodo runner-up) TRS-80 personal computer.

The most exciting development ever chronicled in its pages was the stringy-floppy drive, an astounding device that stored information on "wafers" (skinny microcassettes). The stringy-floppy drive was much faster than the audio cassette but, at under $500, didn't carry the crushing expense associated with floppy disks. Those were heady days.

LOTUS: HAL

Lotus is the Mattel of the software industry. Mattel is Barbie, Hot Wheels, and a huge and constantly changing mix of consistently unwanted other toys. Lotus is 1-2-3 and one unsalable dog after another. This is true today and it was true when Lotus produced HAL.

HAL was to Lotus what Toot Sweet (a machine that made whistles out of Tootsie Rolls, as a movie tie-in to *Chitty Chitty Bang Bang*) was to Mattel: yet another in a long line of losers feeding off the cash cow.

If you don't remember HAL, here's what it did: let you communicate to your spreadsheet in plain English. Written English. That's right. Want to insert a row? Type "insert a row." Want to duplicate a formula? Type "copy C2 to C3:C14, then copy C2:C14 to D2:J14." Using English didn't make spreadsheets any easier to understand, and it also made using them even slower and more tedious. HAL died quietly.

CAUZIN: SOFTSTRIP

This ungainly device could read digital information, encoded in a two-inch-wide smear of square black dots, from the printed page. Cauzin even convinced MacUser to print programs in SoftStrip format for a couple of months. Short programs.

The SoftStrip made a lot of sense, or at least some sense, when computers were popular and modems were expensive oddities. Sadly, that was a pretty short window of opportunity.

THUNDERSCAN

A masterpiece of kludgy engineering, this turned Apple's ImageWriter printer into a surprisingly good scanner. It was just an infrared LED and a photocell in a housing that replaced the printer's ribbon. Coupled with a little software, it would actually do a fairly good high-resolution black-and-white scan of a photograph in about fifteen minutes. And it was cheap!

Another brilliant innovation done in by the laser printer.

MAGNUSON

For a brief moment in the early 1980s, it seemed that the Next Big Thing in the computer industry was going to be the plug-compatible mainframe. Why spend a million bucks on an IBM mainframe when you could get a Magnuson for half as much?

This was a compelling argument for about three years, until the supermini and the PC became common. Then the question on everyone's lips became: Why spend half a million bucks on a mainframe at all?

IBM still exists, sort of. Magnuson doesn't.

BORLAND: TURBO PROLOG

It seemed like a good idea, particularly from the vantage point of the early 1980s, when it seemed like artificial intelligence might turn out to be the Next Big Thing. (See HAL and M.1 above.) Having made a fortune off of Turbo Pascal, a cheap compiler for an almost unusable language that had been invented for teaching computer science students how to program, Borland tried to repeat their success.

What they failed to take into account is that all programming languages are almost unusable. Prolog, however, is completely unusable.

IBM: TOPVIEW

Microsoft Windows without all that graphical-user-interface point-and-click crap. ◆

 *Notes*

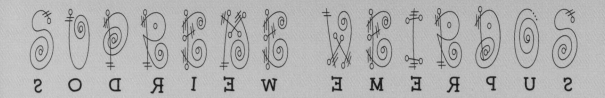

SUPREME WEIRDOS

W hat are the qualities that separate your run-of-the-mill weirdo from the truly supreme variety? First of all, one can't simply "decide" to become a kook. Telling others you're weird, or just wearing a wacky outfit, is a sure giveaway that you're utterly and hopelessly normal. A Supreme Weirdo knows that *everyone else* is weird for being so straight and serious in our funhouse-mirror world.

Just having a bizarre theory isn't enough, either. Everyone harbors a unique explanation for how the world works, but few of us are willing to write it down on a sandwich board and walk around town shouting at people about it.

Having a feverish drive to teach the world your special secret knowledge is enough to make you a plain-vanilla weirdo. But to be a Supreme Weirdo, you've got to be an artist as well. Through self-published art, literature, and guerrilla performance, the Supreme Weirdo is able give us poor sober-brained non-weirdos a glimpse into other realities.

What is it about Supreme Weirdos that's so intriguing? Most of them aren't happy, and many of their ideas go against the very laws of physics, math, and chemistry, and they are usually off-base historically. Why should Happy Mutants care about the kooky theories of such a weirdo?

We don't look to Supreme Weirdos to teach us life's basics, we like them because we get to hitch a free ride on a brain that's broken its tether to rational thought and floats high above the grim world of matter-of-fact, no-fun reality. A good weirdo publication can rival the best sci-fi and comic book; a weirdo's rant can beat anything an avant-garde spoken-word artist can dream up. The Supreme Weirdo may not like your reasons for being interested in them, but chances are, they'll be grateful for the attention anyway. They're usually suckers for it. ◆

Chip Wass

Journey to Kooktopia

by *Gareth Branwyn & Mark Frauenfelder*

"And they knew not their hole from an ass on the ground"
—Firesign Theater
The Book of Holes

The Church of the SubGenius uses the term "Bulldada" to refer to "that which is good because it has no idea how bad it is." While most people might immediately think of kitsch art or The Home Shopping Network as primary sources of bulldada, we recently stumbled across a whole universe of do-it-yourself inventors who put all the art-school surrealists to shame. Imagine this:

You live in a world caught up in an interdimensional/intergalatic war being fought on an infinite number of battle-fronts. A golden age of super-science and psychic wonders—our birthright—has been stolen from us, and only a handful of weekend warriors have

discovered the truth and are brave enough to fight for it. The very laws of physics (among other things) are at stake. Free energy, immortality, space-time travel, and the ability to hack the very laws of thermodynamics should all be available to us. So what's gummed up the perpetual engine of progress?

In the bulldada universe next door, the enemy goes by many names: The Elite, the Men In Black, the Illuminati, the Shadow Government, the Gnomes of Zurich. Whatever they're called, you can blame them for the gravity dump we currently live on. They're the ones who've bought or stolen Utopia's blueprints and shelved them in the dusty safes of old government buildings, or sold them to the Soviets, or slipped them to bug-eyed monsters through gaping holes in space-time. Composed of a flagitious

alliance between corrupt humans and evil space aliens, the Elite is hell-bent on keeping the working stiffs of the world (that's YOU) addicted to petroleum, pesticides, and pharmaceuticals—all products of greedy global corporations who've signed pacts with the Shadow Empire.

The Russkies are key players in this unholy alliance, too. For years, the Russians have been blasting massive doses of electromagnetic energy into our skulls with enormous transmitters. These waves are eating away at our brains, corrupting our morals, and preventing us from realizing what's really going on (please see above). Recently, the world-dominating shadow-elite-alien-commie-government-conspiracy has us believing that they aren't the same one-world-and-we'll-bury-you freaks they've always been. So now that our guard is down, they're

about to initiate Phase Two of their dastardly plan—triggering cyclopean earthquakes across North America by resonating geomagnetic polarity bands.

And, as if all this wasn't enough, we've also got the "independents" to deal with, such as the Deros, a race of sinister dwarves living in honeycombed tunnels throughout the Earth's crust, and bee-like Martians with Mensa-level IQs who buzz their tiny saucers over our sleepy Spielbergian neighborhoods. Some of the Earth's quixotic protectors believe that the Earth and its inhabitants are actually owned by an alien race that has "a legal right to us, by force, or by having paid out analogues of beads for us to former, more primitive owners." (Charles Fort)

But fear thee not! For there is amassing, in the garages and foreclosed farmlands of America, a fearless army of self-educated stalwarts standing at the gates of the Elite's citadel. They have designed and built awesome weapons and bewildering gizmos to fight (or at least puzzle to death) the Shadowy forces that threaten us. Armed with glass bulbs filled with exotic Tesla gases, gyroscopes, redesigned AC generators, polar negative discs run by vibratory circuits of sympathetic polar attraction drawn directly from space, and ether pumps,

they are going to demolish the tyrants who have turned the human race into a bunch of slaves and mind-mutilated cattle.

They are the kook-tech inventors and salesmen and this is their story. So snuggle up in your Orgone Blanket, fix yourself a mug of hydrogen peroxide, crank up the UFO detector, and read on!

FRY ME TO THE MOON
"Curiosity is a sighn [sic] of intelligence"
—Al Fry

Al Fry, who lives in a one-payphone town in Idaho, is the proprietor of Fry's Incredible Inquiries, a mail-order business of D.I.Y. kooktech manuals, books on UFOs and the coming new age. As an expert on suppressed inventions and the owner of "probably the largest selection of time travel publications ever put together," Fry told us that some of his customers "go backwards and forwards using these machines." Fry hesitated to give us much information about time travel: "I only go so far in most of my interest and dealings in such areas due to the dangers involved. Big Brother keeps tabs on the really high-tech geniuses around and I prefer to remain just enough of the country boy to slow such problems." Fry claims that the most advanced high-tech gadgetry has been around for ten thousand years, but that the common folk have lost access to it. "The government & 'elite' front men have technology that is pretty

mind boggling but I can't get any deeper than I am," said a cautious Fry.

Fry is more willing to discuss Project Phoenix, which began as a government-run weather balloon program that unleashed a Pandora's box of psychic disaster upon the citizens. The most benign function of the balloons was to transmit a Wilhelm Reich–discovered radio frequency that reduced the intensity of storms by attracting Orgone, and disrupting DOR (Deadly Orgone). But the transmissions were also "pulsed & cycled" in such a way as to control the minds of people living under the influence of the balloons. The same signals, when intensified, were used to generate time warp vortices large enough to send an automobile and its hapless occupants careening through time. The scientists continued to increase the strength of the Reichian waves until giant mental constructs were unleashed and could not be contained. Around 1983, the constructs coalesced and took the form of a 25-foot-tall Bigfoot monster, wreaking havoc and terrorizing project scientists. Some feel that the monster was created by a renegade faction of the government who wanted to sabotage Project Phoenix for their own wicked purposes.

Fry is an authority on everything from the dangers of ice cream ("Smelly, chemical-laden poison that we wouldn't even feed our dog. In its frozen form with its artificial 'taste foolers' it gets spooned right down our gullets.") to proper living for trailer park denizens ("The aluminum sends deleterious rays inward which is unhealthy and draining. Polarity devices and such are of some benefit. One self-made device consists of a pan of sand that is charged up under a properly made pyramid. Set in a corner this works for around a wee . . . at which time some cold unpolluted water should be poured over the sand & its wood container to cleanse it.")

Fry also offers a correspondence course in Human Functioning Secrets that makes this modest claim: "Once you have taken the full course, you should be able to mind read, stop your mental and physical pain as well as showing others how to do so, have a total memory recall, share beauty in relationships, talk a new communication, know the answers to hate, pride, prejudice and hostility, have a true knowledge of world peace and a serenity never known before. You will have answers to miracles, the beginning of time, what infinity is, how it happened and what you really are. You will have a new communication with nature and all living beings."

ELECTRONIC WITCHCRAFT

John Ernst Worrell Keely, born in 1827, was a guy who gave garage inventors a bad name. He claimed to have discovered a new physical force that resulted from the intermolecular vibration of ether. This sympathetic vibratory action could be used to drive an engine. After Keely demonstrated a prototype of his motor, he was able to obtain investors and the Keely Motor Company was born. Subsequently, Keely was unable to perfect his motor or to patent the device. He continued to get funding for his projects even though none of his devices ever worked outside of his physical presence. Devotees even claim that he had the devices tuned to his body so that only he could operate them. When he died, officers of the Keely Motor Company had his workshop thoroughly examined. They found numerous trapdoors, air and hydraulic lines, and other sideshow trickery. Keely was summarily denounced as a fraud.

But Jerry Decker and the other folks at Vangard Sciences don't want to be confused by the "facts." They run KeelyNet (a popular bulletin board in Kooktopia), host conferences, and put out a newsletter, all devoted to Keely and such related voodoo-tech as levitation, radionics, anti-grav machines, and UFOs. They say Keely was one of the great scientists of our age and that he was the victim, like all free energy crusaders, of greed, power, and ego. "It always boils down to these three things," says Decker. "Keely was so far ahead of his time, they haven't even begun to figure out what he was about. Read your quantum physics and you'll see how right Keely was." When asked about the 1884 *Scientific American* article that revealed the workshop scam, Decker makes light of it, chalking it up once again to ego, power, and greed. We ask him the obvious question of why no free energy device has ever been found to withstand the test of time (or even close examination). If any of this were real, wouldn't greed, power, and ego also compel a corporation to want to get there first and corner one of these discoveries? And, doesn't the radionic pendulum swing both ways? Couldn't ego, power, and greed just be a teensy-weensy reason why the inventors tinker with this stuff in the first place? He freely admits that lots of the free energy inventors are "a bit crazy, paranoid, egotistical, and greedy," but he refuses to suspect the integrity of their ideas.

As we talk, Decker gets more and more excited. We ask him about Scalar Beam weapons, and in seconds he leaps back to the Middle Ages, to something posited then called "first issue," a clear fluid that leaks out of you when your skin is broken. He goes into frenzied detail about how this substance continues to have a sympathetic relationship with you after it leaves your body. He suggests an experiment. The next time someone cuts themselves, put the "first issue" on a swab and take it to another room. Don't tell your now profusely bleeding subject what you are doing. If you, from the other room, pour alcohol onto the swab, the person will feel it on their wound. Decker is off on the next subject before we can ask him if he's ever tried it. He seems startled by

the question. No, he hasn't. Does he know anyone who has tried it? Several of his friends did and nothing happened. But, let him tell us about this other neat thing he read ("All this is available on KeelyNet, by the way.") that says iatrogenic diseases in hospitals can be explained by this sympathetic ooze theory. All the bandages in the hospital are thrown in the same hamper where your diseased ooze oozes all over everybody else's first ooze. These icky mutant disease vibes are then beamed backed to you, and all viral hell breaks loose. Bulldada!

From here Decker careens off into the fourth dimension with some nonsense about taking snapshots of scalar waveforms of various diseases and then beaming the disease pattern back into other people. He says some papers on KeelyNet describe how the Soviets were doing this for years, aiming their deadly scalar waves toward Oregon. And then AIDS, the ultimate disease for paranoids, enters the conversation. Yup . . . that's right . . . scalar beams.

KeelyNet's pièce de résistance is Decker's own essay on the Krell Helmet. Remember the movie Forbidden Planet and the long-dead Krells, whose engines of progress still hummed in immense canyons of steel beneath the planet? The Krell Helmet was a device that the civilization had built to pump up their big alien brains. Decker claims a friend of a friend of a friend (no foolin') has built such a device and that this "engineering genius" now has mental muscle to spare. He can enter into other people's brains to read their thoughts or seed them. He can extend his "cerebellic fields" to control mass for "genetic transmutation, levitation, and a host of other unknown possibilities." "I can't really tell you any more than that. I know a lot more, but I'm not at liberty to divulge. [He starts giggling.] I can tell you the guy is kinda kinky [more giggling]. He almost killed his girlfriend with a helmet. They had sex while he was wearing it and . . . ya know . . . it amplifies everything. [Snicker snicker.]"

HURLER OF LIGHTNING

If Keely is the mischievous angel of Kooktopia, Tesla is the risen god. His research and inventions in electricity and radio are fundamental to much of our technology today. Many of his speculations about satellites, microwaves, robotics, and his "world system of intelligence transmission" (interconnected radio, telephone, personal communications and information services) have proven to be very prescient. Even Star Wars, tele-robotic wars of science fought in space, was a Tesla prediction. His personal eccentricities, his strange working methods (he allegedly prototyped in his mind) and his penchant for making outrageous claims (such as stating that he could split the Earth in two like an apple and that he spoke with ETs) have made him a primary object of worship in kook circles. Those who study him and his inventions mix his scientifically sound discoveries with his wackier speculations. They seem to make very little attempt to critically evaluate his work. If Tesla thought it, it must be true.

Enter Steve Elswick and his magazine *Extraordinary Science*, the official publication of the International Tesla Society. This quarterly publication reports on the doings of the society and their Colorado Springs Tesla Museum. *Extraordinary Science* also publishes papers which cover the gamut of Tesla-tech from the practical to the downright daffy. Recent issues spend a lot of time discussing electro-healing therapies, with many of the references cited being from turn-of-the-century publications! Kirlian photography, Rife Plasma Beams, and other "light therapies" are uncritically discussed. Evaluative data is given short shrift over anecdotal comments such as this from an article on the Violet Ray healing device: " . . . We use it, and we've noticed that the problems seem to clear up for us faster than people who don't use the device." The author notes that the most dramatic effect is on the family dog and his stiff back: "We apply the electrode to his back for less than thirty seconds, and within an hour the stiffness always disappears." Other themes in *Extraordinary Science* include UFOs, free energy systems, and various speculative theories about the nature of natural forces.

STRANGE LOOPS

When we started on our journey through Kooktopia, we used dada and surrealism as convenient signposts. Now that we're done looking at the map, it looks more like a work of deconstructionism. To these wacky tinkerers, science is a story, a collection of good cosmo-conceptions buttressed by a few anecdotes and some hot rumors. If it sounds good, it is good. The sketches, the diagrams, and the patents do not refer to anything, they are the thing itself. The more complex and arcane the drawing, the more ancient the knowledge, the more powerful the "discovery." Experimentation becomes performance (to lure in other scientists and investors). Several people we talked to even suggested, in answer to questions of fraud, that their colleagues might sometimes need to fake a demo due to the sensitive nature of their device and the pressures of making the tech work on cue. It's not surprising that a number of well-known kook inventors worked in the circus or vaudeville before they went into *serious* science.

There is a logic applied in this world of funhouse science that defies self-criticism. It is very similar to the Mobius-looped philosophy of fringe science's big sister, the New Age. If something goes wrong with the technology, it's because of some outside force (weather conditions, faulty parts, sabotage). It's never the fundamental principles on which the design is based or the design itself that is at fault. And if the U.S. Patent Office rejects an application, it must be because there is a suppressive conspiracy at work. Countless individuals experimenting with etheric forces or Keely's vibratory physics and making no appreciable headway have not dissuaded new generations of kooktechs from trying all over again. The fact that it doesn't work has only magnified its attraction— this is a magical world and these people are questing for philosopher stones.

Of course, in the end, the last laugh may be on those of us who hold on to such stuffy notions as the Laws of Thermodynamics and who are immediately skeptical of etheric forces, free energy devices, and build-it-yourself UFOs. After all, science is not immutable. New ways of looking at things, new discoveries, can radically change our thinking. Recent studies in chaos and dynamical systems are a case in point. And if one of these contraptions does pan out, we'd be more than happy to parade around with "pyramid energizers" on our heads and confess our ignorance. Maybe you have to be as crazy as Tesla (who puked at the sight of round objects) to come up with the AC generator, or as whacked as Newton (who allegedly couldn't stand the sight of female pubic hair) to invent the calculus, or as tweaked as Edison (who named his kids Dot and Dash) to invent the light bulb and the phonograph. Maybe it's not such a bad idea to be tolerant of even the grossest techno-whoey. Remember, one of today's kooks could turn out to be tomorrow's hero of science. ◆

RESOURCES: PASSPORT TO KOOKTOPIA

We barely visited a barrio of the vast Kooktopian environs. Contact these travel guides for the full packaged tour:

Al Fry's Incredible Inquiry Catalog
HC 76, Box 2207,
Garden Valley, ID 83622.
(Free)

KeelyNet
PO Box 1031, Mesquite, TX 75150
BBS 214/324-3501
(Free)

Extraordinary Science
International Tesla Society
330-A West Uintah St., Ste. 215,
Colorado Springs, CO 80905-1095.
$25/year.

Klark Kent's Super Science
Box 392, Dayton, OH 45409.
(A treasure-trove of bulldada objets d'art. UFO Detector $239. $5 for info pack.)

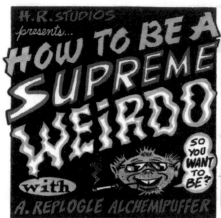

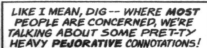

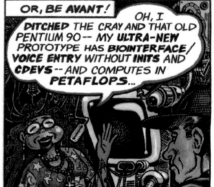

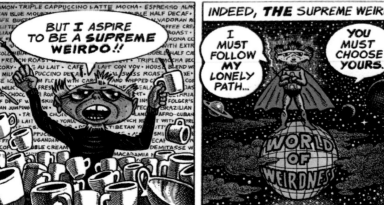

Lamprey Systems:

Mark Frauenfelder

Software That Sucks!

Ninety-nine percent of all computer programs can be thrown onto one of four piles: communications, business, games, or education. While useful, such programs bore me. It's that tiny *fifth* pile of software containing the remaining 1 percent that I like to sift through. It's here that I find programs that surprise me in some way. One of my favorite "fifth-pile" software companies is Boise, Idaho–based Lamprey Systems.

Why are Lamprey products so special? I think it's because their products are fun to use AND they don't contain the standard genre cliches other computer games rely on. Lamprey programs are satirical simulations of modern-day life, with special emphasis on making fun of mass media. I'd much rather sit down with a copy of Lamprey's *Geraldo-Matic* than *DOOM* or *Mortal Kombat*. *Geraldo-Matic* is a trash-TV show generator in which you play the guest and must answer host Geraldo Reararea's questions, such as "What advice do you have for other passive-aggressive sex addicts in search of serial killers who are interested in freebasing?" All the while, an unflattering image of a bloated, wide-eyed Geraldo grimaces, screeches, and burps.

After playing with *Geraldo-Matic* and other Lamprey titles, such as *MacJesus* (a personal savior on a floppy) and *Haikook* (classical Japanese haiku for white trash), I began wondering about the company that made them and about the brilliant men and women who must work there. What kind of brains did they have throbbing in their craniums? I was just burning to find out.

I gleaned Lamprey's mailing address from the package of their recent product, *F*CK 'EM*, and wrote, requesting an interview. About a week later, I received a letter on Lamprey letterhead stating that the president,

Robert Carr, would be available for a telephone interview. I called immediately.

To my surprise, Carr himself answered the telephone. It turns out that he is the sole proprietor of Lamprey Systems!

Another surprise: While talking with Carr, I discovered that he's a humble and gentle soul. His phone vibes convey the warmth of an old friend. Talking to him made me feel like Floyd the Barber shooting the breeze with Andy Griffith. This is in sharp contrast to the manic smart-ass attitude infused in Lamprey's software titles, which would lead one to guess that their creator is either an obnoxious screamer or an arrogant gloater. Carr's self-deprecating wit is built into the name of his company. A lamprey is a parasitic, primitive eel with a round sucking mouth equipped with many sharp teeth—hence the company motto: "Software that sucks!"

Robert Carr got his start as a producer of mind-warping media back in those scary Reagan years by publishing *Smurfs in Hell*, a drugs, guns, and anarchy humor zine that wasn't afraid to make fun of anything. One page of an issue might feature doctored magazine ads, such as "Baby's First UZI Bronze Plated in Solid Metal" or "Sex Toys for Christians—Inflatable Virgin Mary Doll: She's hot and holy, and she's ready for immaculate conception!" Another page might list the top ten Shuttle *Challenger* hits: "Bits and Pieces," "Ship of Fools," "Light My Fire," "Whole Lotta Shakin' Going On," etc.

The first few issues of *Smurfs in Hell* were made in the pre-Macintosh dark ages, using a typewriter, and were embellished with crude, but hilarious, line drawings. Later on, Carr forked over his life savings for a Macintosh. His purchase turned out to be a life-changing decision. "I immediately became fascinated by what was going on when I realized that an average Joe Blow could write programs," he says. "I saw Mike Sainz's *MacPlaymate* (a computer sex kitten who will perform various erotic acts at the click of a mouse) making the rounds, and thought of all the wacky and strange possibilities for computers. Then I saw the *Leather Goddesses of Phobos* game (from commercial game manufacturer Infocom) and thought it sucked. When I discovered a small ad for *WorldBuilder* (software that can be used to make your own games) I decided to see if I could do better."

One of Carr's first commercially available products was called *Mormonoids from the Deep*. The object of the game is to kill Idaho Mormon zombies as they emerge from a swamp. Carr sent out "zillions of demo copies" to commercial game companies in an attempt to get distribution, but didn't hit pay dirt. "The legitimate distributors said they liked it," Carr explains, "but couldn't use it because of the content." So, in his typical do-it-yourself fashion, Carr started the Private Idaho BBS in 1991 to distribute his programs.

I asked Carr if he received hate mail from people offended by having their religion or moral code made the object of digital shenanigans. "Not really," he says. "A couple of Mormons actually wrote me and told me they enjoyed my game."

Even though computer stores won't carry Lamprey System titles, there's a loyal underground following that greedily slurps up all of the zany, hormonally-charged software Carr can produce. Carr's long string of hits include *MacWanker* (a dirty phrase generator), *Porno Writer* (which automatically generates satirical *Penthouse Forum*–style stories of sexual experiences), and the *Ed Norton Utilities*: "A sleazy little program I wrote that pretends to evaluate your Mac. It has the lowest of capabilities. It says that your computer is fucked up and to send it to me at my PO box. I haven't scored any hardware yet."

Carr hasn't had any luck finding a major software company to distribute these programs, either. "Game companies have approached me. A guy wanted to distribute *Porno Writer*, but like all the other deals, it fell through. Another time, a university English professor hired me to write a game for the Idaho Centennial. He gave me loose guidelines. I could do anything I wanted as long as it wasn't absolutely filthy. So I made *MacSpud*: a future-Idaho game where you have to haul potatoes to ethanol plants to be converted into fuel. You have to contend with vicious mutant Jackalopes and dodge rockets launched from free-fire zone hunters. It was the cleanest game I wrote and the worst seller."

Even *F*CK 'EM*, Carr's flagship product, doesn't bring in enough money for him to be able to bail out of his day job at the local Kinko's. "Lamprey is not a get-rich-quick operation," he says. "It's nice to get $50 a week, and when *Wired* ran an article about me, I got $1,000 in orders and was able to buy a new Mac." (Previously, all of Carr's programs were produced on a tiny-screened black-and-white Mac SE.)

So if the bucks aren't there, what keeps Carr going? "Positive feedback, a teeny bit of money, fun. I'd be a writer if I had my choice, but you don't get published anymore. I see people copying their 500-page manuscripts at Kinko's and it costs $25 per copy. I can put my programs on a 35-cent floppy or put them online and send them all over the world."

If Carr was given enough dough to produce a commercial game, would he do it? "Yes, I'd be able to blow off Kinko's. But it'd be hard to resist evil ideas. As it stands, I have complete freedom. It's like when your doctor says you have terminal cancer. It kind of sucks, but you can do anything you want!" ◆

Lamprey Systems:
PO Box 2761 Borah Station, Boise, ID 83701. Send e-mail to Carr at smurfboy@aol.com for a complete catalog and product information. Private Idaho BBS: 208/338-9227.

Patch Adams: Why Be Normal?

Gareth Branwyn

Patch Adams, M.D., likes to make trouble. Wherever he goes, whatever he does, he generates controversy and inspires a raw form of hope. He's big, he's loud, he's extremely intelligent. He'd probably be terrifying if he weren't so disarmingly friendly. Both a family physician and a professional clown, Patch travels the world lecturing on health care and his community-based hospital (called the Gesundheit Institute) in West Virginia. Few people can resist his wacky antics and his genuine desire to help people enjoy their lives more. A major studio is currently planning a motion picture based on Patch's life. Patch has a mail fetish. Write him at: The Gesundheit Institute, 6877 Washington Blvd., Arlington, VA 22213. ◆

Photos by Holton Rower

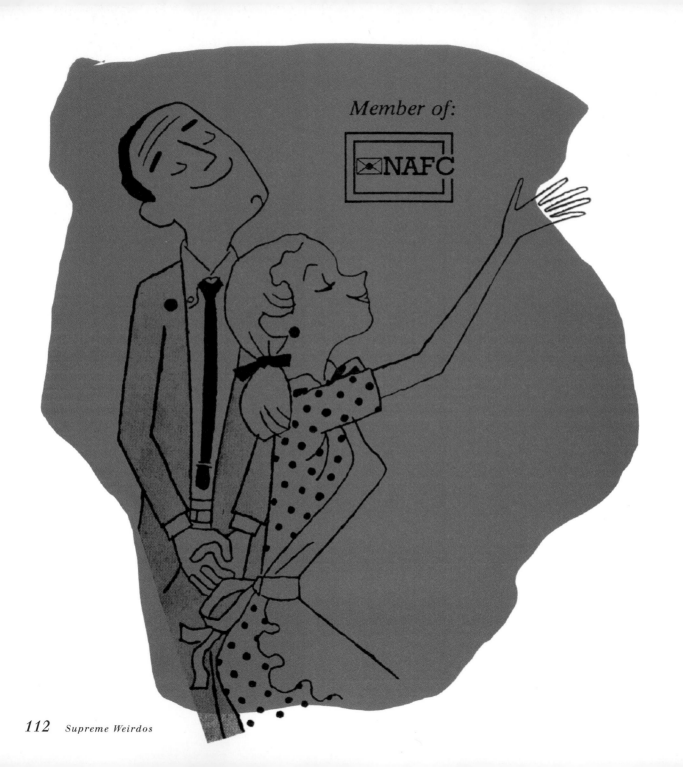

Member of:

⬛✉NAFC

Are Fan Club Presidents

Nuts?

-or-

THE TORTURED, RIDICULED, UNAPPRECIATED
LIFE OF A FAN CLUB PRESIDENT

Marjorie Ingall

One might think they'd all be hyperventilating teenage girls with no self-awareness and no self-esteem, blinded by devotion for their idols. But no, the reality of fan club presidents is far more complex. I talked to three and discovered that their motives for running the clubs, their awareness of how non-fans perceived them, even their attitudes toward the objects of their affection, differed widely.

THE GEORGE STEPHANOPOULOS FAN CLUB

P.O. Box 9804, Stanford, CA 94039
pollyfab@well.com

George's duckiest all-time fans are these two foxy market-oriented liberals named Polly and Michael. They started their club as business-school students at Stanford. They are very self-aware little pumpkins, and while their official club organ (ahem), *Stephanopouletter*, is hilariously dizzy with minutiae and

lust for the taste treat that is the wee senior policy advisor, they are quite savvy about what they're doing. They fully expect to make money (they did go to business school, after all), "and we thought we could achieve wacky fame," says Michael, 31. Both he and Polly, 29, once roamed the corridors of political power themselves, Michael with DC's foreign service office and Polly with Paul Simon's presidential campaign. They are actually optimistic about government's ability to help people (hello?), and George is an integral part of their delusion.

The idea for the club sprang full-blown from their wee Ivy League heads at a dinner party in 1992, when the conversation turned to the universal fascination with George. "He was so successful it was amazing, yet he didn't seem that different from us," says Michael, in hushed and reverent tones. "There was a strong interest and a pleasant envy in what he'd accomplished. His cuteness is a nice add-on, but not the whole thing; it's the job. If he were a Republican he would not have that kind of response. So we got the idea of starting a fan club." It currently has about 200 members, including George's mother.

The tone of the *Stephanopouletter* is simultaneously adoring and ironic. One gets the sense that the GSFC is both a fan club and a parody of a fan club. No element of George's persona is too minute to obsess over. In a recent issue, a member named Kris optimistically shares her certainty that George does not have a back hair problem. John B., "a bitter young man who may be just a tad jealous," maliciously tells of watching George

get bested in a "daring, intense and oh-so-silent competition of pedaling" with an aerobics instructor on an exercise bike in a health club. His glee prompts Polly and Michael to editorialize: "Gee, John B., that was not such a favorable story. We can only print such a tale because we know that our readers will see the evil in you, not George." The newsletter offers astrologically compatible matchups for George (Cicely Tyson, yes! Jennifer Grey, no!) and opportunities to purchase the exclusive line of GS fan club clothing.

M and P met their idol after he read of their devotion in *People* magazine and sent them "a cute, embossed card" inviting them to the White House. The meeting took place under the disapproving fish-eyed gaze of Stephanopoulos's humorless and overly possessive assistant, Miss Heather Beckel (who has blocked my every attempt at interviewing her lord and master). This did not dim Michael and Polly's ardor, though Michael thought George's nose looked funny in person.

Mikey is quite articulate about the reasons for his evangelism. To him, George stands for something larger than Georgeness, embodying the progressive yet not blindly idealistic political agenda of many twentysome-things. "Our peppy, fun-filled and hopeful values fly in the face of current conven-tional wisdom about the supposedly slacker, Generation X existence,"

Michael writes. "Fear not, oh enthusiastic and full-of-life fan, we are ready to take this larger message about the revival of the post-Reagan generation on the road!" I can't wait.

THE SLIM WHITMAN APPRECIATION SOCIETY OF THE U.S.

(S.W.A.S., founded 1970). 1002 W. Thurber St., Tucson, AZ 85705.

Slim Whitman's fan club prez, Loren Knapp, is less ironic about his proclivity. His love for the mustached, yodeling, sequined-suit-and-cowboy-hat-sporting country singer dates back to 1968. "I was standing in my sister's kitchen and she had the radio on. And this voice singing 'How Great Thou Art' came out of the radio—it was my mother's favorite hymn—and I just stopped in my tracks. Because it was just magnificent; it was incredible. The way it would just slide into a falsetto could make the hair on the back of your neck stand up, it's that beautiful. So I called the radio station and they said, 'That's Slim Whitman!'"

Loren quickly became the American correspondent for the British Slim Whitman Appreciation Society. In 1970, he started the American chapter. The society deliberately eschews the term "fan club," and its associations with "women getting all excited, jumping up and down in poodle skirts." This is a more sober appreciation of Mr. Whitman's 127 albums (who knew?), his history of touring the deep South with Elvis Presley in the '50s, his stature

as singer of the all-time best-selling TV-marketed album in history. Surely you remember: In 1980, Suffolk Marketing (of Ginsu knife fame) began running TV commercials for the *Slim Whitman: All My Best* album. You may recall the opening image of Slim singing "Una Paloma Blanca" in a courtyard, yodeling surreally. "He lip-synched it at 2 A.M. in a studio in Philadelphia," Loren says, with the air of one passing

along an oft-told ancient Norse saga. "It sold at least 1.2 million copies in the first two weeks. No one's done that, including Elvis and Boxcar Willie. Kids had never heard a sliding falsetto that could take your breath away. I mean, the man can yodel for 49 seconds!"

Today Mr. Knapp, 47, works for the Arizona State Lottery, running the fan club out of his dining room. He is

My TOP 10
Michael Pare
films

What are yours?

NRS KATHY MC FADDEN
-England-

1. Sunset Heat
2. Empire City *
3. Streets of Fire
4. Instant Justice
5. Eddie and The Cruisers
6. Eddie and The Cruisers II
7. Blink of an Eye
8. Into The Sun
9. The Philadelphia Experiment
10. The Women's Club

* Overseas fans and
Japanese fans have the advantage
here, as USA fans have not had
the opportunity to see EMPIRE
CITY. It was released in
theaters overseas, but has
been released in the US

It's available on video
side the US) by Warner
Video.

and it sent chills up and down her spine and brought such warm, glowing feelings to her body, and she just had the urge to get better—this is the reason I do this." Amen.

THE MICHAEL PARE FAN CLUB
(formerly Michael Pare Advocates)
PO Box 307, Savoy, IL 61874
Where Knapp gets cranky at Slim Whitman's lesser listeners, who don't know the meaning of true fandom, Gretchen Felix gets cranky at the very star she purports to worship. Felix, 56, is a former high-ranking official in the Jack Lord fan club. Now she devotes her attentions to Michael Pare. Mr. Pare is perhaps best known in this country for his lead role in the rock flick *Eddie and the Cruisers*, which also made fleeting stars of Springsteen-manqués John Cafferty and the Beaver Brown Band. In Japan, though, Pare is inexplicably a huge underground star. Pare's Japanese fan club is funded by JVC, the electronics giant, which supplies office space, supplies, and advertising. It has 3,000 members and the muscle to run Pare's failed 1986–'87 American TV series *Houston Nights* on Japanese TV and to demand Michael Pare movie marathons at local theaters so members can sit through *Eddie and the Cruisers* 8 or 9 times in a row. Merely mentioning the Japanese club can send Gretchen into a tight-lipped fury. She struggles to keep the 50 members she has, and

working on compiling a 50-page discography, producing a Slim newsletter, placing ads in country music magazines, calling radio stations to request Slim's songs. The legend's inability to get airplay, while the Travis Tritts and Billy Ray Cyruses have their 15 minutes, disgusts him. So do self-termed fans who fail to give back to the stars they purport to worship. "All they want is 'Gimme, gimme, gimme. Oh, I'm your biggest fan, I love you to death, send me an autographed picture!' They want stuff, but they don't want to belong. They don't want

to help. People are not joiners," he concludes sadly. And those who do join can be fickle. "They buy a few albums and disappear. I'm like, 'What did I do wrong, as the president? Was it something I wrote? Did I alienate them?" The membership has fallen from a high of 700 to about 350, but Knapp is undeterred. His wife is irked by his time-consuming passion ("I have to turn it off when she comes in the room"), but he is unbowed.

"Look," he says earnestly. "When you get a letter from a woman who's really ill, and she saw that commercial she's at least $1,500 in the hole at any given time.

When I called Celebrity Service, the organization that keeps track of stars' agents and managers, they directed me to Creative Artists Agency. When I called them, I learned that as of July 1994, Michael was no longer represented by CAA. He had no representation in America, period. He was living in Amsterdam, they thought. Uh, they weren't sure if he was still working. (Actually, he's doing low-budget Italian and Israeli action films.) I said "Actually, I was calling about the Michael Pare Fan Club. Do you know how I could—" The woman on the other end of the phone cut me off with a bloodcurdling shriek. "Ohmigod! She made my life a living hell! She used to call and demand to know Michael's favorite color RIGHT NOW, or the newsletter wouldn't go out and Michael's popularity would suffer! She's nuts! Ask her about the Japanese fan club!"

Gretchen is not nuts. She's devoted. She is deadly serious, speaking in a slowly measured, low-pitched voice. "Eight years ago we moved from Phoenix [hmm—what is it about fan club presidents and the fertile soil of Phoenix?] to a small university town and I needed something to occupy my time. I don't know how I latched on to Michael. He had some of the qualities of my son in his comedy roles, and he was like a brother I'd lost some years ago at about the same age. He'd had

charisma unlike anyone else, and he was shy but quite sincere, like Michael. He was a private person, and Michael is also." Gretchen's brother committed suicide, and maybe her devotion and loyalty to Michael is an attempt to rescue her brother retroactively. "We stick by Michael no matter what, through the most horrible films; we know he's completely underrated by *Hollywood*." Gretchen snarls the very word.

Still, she's bitter because Pare shows so little interest in the activities of his own club. "He gives no input or feedback on his career. He doesn't want his privacy disturbed. I've been told you shouldn't do this unless you have personal contact with your celebrity. It's frustrating. I know Michael's married for the third time, but I don't know when he got married. It isn't documented. Almost nothing

has been printed since 1990. I presently have no address for his fan mail. I have a number to get information about him; I leave messages, but no one ever calls back. They just answer, 'law office.'"

Despite such brief flashes of anger, Gretchen's faithfulness seems almost noble. In her patient, confident wait for her hero's return to triumph, she reminds me of Penelope, waiting for Odysseus. Instead of weaving and unraveling a tapestry over and over, she plugs recycled data into her laptop—ancient headshots and vintage clippings of long-since-gone-straight-to-video movies. Don't laugh. Such loyalty is rare now.

So, wanna start your own fan club? Call the National Association of Fan Clubs, 818/763-3280. For 5 bucks they'll send you a nifty how-to book. Course, you can always ignore the rules and do it yourself! ♦

Ivan Stang:

Sacred Scribe of the Church

of the SubGenius

Rudy Rucker

"Repent! Quit your jobs! Slack off!"
—*The Book of the SubGenius*

*T*he Church of the SubGenius was founded over twenty years ago by a gang of genius nerd misfit filmmakers, writers, and underground cartoonists from Dallas and San Francisco. The church celebrates the power of the individual weirdo and mocks the mind-set and behavior of the masses, whom church members dub the "Pinks."

The secret power of a SubGenius, as explained by their assassinated (and undoubtedly fictional) savior, J. R. "Bob" Dobbs, is the Yeti-blood that courses through the bloodstreams of all members of the church. Pinks have no Yeti ancestors, and because of this, they cannot help being the unwitting tools of a grand conspiracy.

Anyone, however, Pink or not, can become a fully-ordained minister of the Church of the SubGenius by sending $20 to The SubGenius Foundation, PO Box 140360, Dallas, TX 75124. Or send $1 for some propaganda leaflets.
—Editors

IVAN STANG: Don't interview me. The article should be about the Church of the SubGenius, not about me. I'm just a part of the Church, though definitely the hardest working part. I want to keep it clear that "Bob" comes first, not me.

RUDY RUCKER: *I've turned away from Christianity and I often feel a lack in my life these days, Ivan. Can "Bob" actually fill the hunger for religion?*

No, he can't. It's really your own amazing interior brain doing all the trick special effects. "Bob" is but the cheapest PATH. You don't have to believe in anything—only "Yoko and me," so to speak.

One thing that makes me not take "Bob" completely seriously is that when I'm in a hospital thinking I might die, I feel more like praying to Jesus than to "Bob."
There's nothing wrong with repenting on your deathbed. It's all a "just in case" thing anyway. Most of those people, it's

not that they love God so much, it's that they love the idea of YOU burning in Hell for eternity. Pray to Jesus just in case there's an afterlife. Pray to "Bob" just in case there's an X-Day and the saucers come to kill all the Normals.

When is X-day?
July 5, 1998, 7 o'clock in the morning —starting at the International Date Line, in the middle of the Pacific Ocean. California will be one of the last Earth places ruptured. There, you can watch X-day on TV for nearly a

full day before it hits you. Watching X-day in progress may be "Bob's" biggest test of faith. You may not like what you see. The Ruptured SubGenii will resemble self-immolated Vietnamese monks. You may feel like burning your Church of the SubGenius membership card. But it won't do any good . . .

What about the Church's latest book, Revelation X?
Our first book, *The Book of the SubGenius,* showed the glory that is

"Bob." It offered more sheer, unflinching bullshit than the *Book of Mormon*. But *Revelation X* shows the *danger* that is "Bob." Thanks to our art director Paul Mavrides, it's really really sick; it makes the first book look like a Jehovah's Witness pamphlet or a Jack Chick comic book by comparison.

What did you do over the summer?
I went to DragonCon in Atlanta, which was great, a science-fiction convention, they paid me. And they had Sister Susie the Floozie. She's our latest professional SubGenius preacher and she's great, a very talented writer. She's an ex-stripper.

Did you fuck her?
(*Outraged.*) Why do you even have to ask that?? I haven't fucked her and I wouldn't. I'm married, and if I did fuck the Flooze, I sure as hell wouldn't tell *you*. I *have* hefted her tits, though, her bare nekkid tits; they're all any red-blooded hetero American guy could ask for, I promise you. She preaches rather vividly about her personal experiences with Connie Dobbs, "Bob's" primary wife. After DragonCon I preached a pagan event called Starwood, held in far western rural New York. Tim Leary and Terence McKenna and Robert Anton Wilson are other frequent guest speakers there. I run across those guys frequently. The greatest of the drug-addled philosophers . . . they always bum cigarettes from me.

Were you stoned?
(*Increasingly testy.*) I never fool with cheap conspiracy street drugs when I'm working. After the show, that's a whole different thing. The kind of things I end up taking are still legal, however. Toad venom and Hawaiian Baby Woodrose Seed and San Pedro Cactus . . . I took some of that at Starwood. It's an aphrodisiac, like yohimbe. Instant and perpetual hard-on. Of course my wife wasn't there, so I had to sit in my tent and beat off.

Describe your childhood and adolescence.

Well. I'd say the main aspects were my Mammy and Pappy, The Three Stooges, and Bugs Bunny. I had pretty much of a rationalist upbringing. My parents quit going to church when the preacher told them they shouldn't drink. I got pretty good grades, read monster comics, and H. G. Wells—just what you'd think of as "the typical SubGenius," although that's a contradiction in terms. I even drew comics, but when I was 12, I ritualistically burned all these hundreds of comics I had drawn, because we were moving to a new town (Dallas) and I had decided I wasn't going to be weird anymore. I decided I was going to be normal. Luckily, this idiotic change of heart didn't take.

Something must have happened in high school?
I'd been making 8mm monster movies since I was ten, trying to be the next Ray Harryhausen, the stop-motion animation genius. By the time I got to high school I was winning awards for these claymation films I'd made. I was already a celebrity and a has-been by the time I was eighteen. I'd won awards all over the world. But as my old boss Brownie Brownrigg used to say, "Awards don't taste good even with ketchup."

What really happened in high school —I hit puberty at the age of 5, honest, and by age 12, I was an absolute sex fiend. I was really ready for female companionship, but my parents put

"I can't believe I opened this book."

We can. You did it because it looked **different.** Most other people *avoided* it for that very reason. Maybe . . . just maybe . . . YOU are as "DIFFERENT" as this book is. You *seek out* the "different," *for its own sake,* and that odd trait of yours has led you now to peruse this "funny book."

Or has it?

What if some catalyst stronger than your engramatic programming, more powerful than the combined forces of the spirit-world, *compelled* you to pick it up and begin reading? Just took control of your body, mind and soul and got you to Page 2 before easing back in the cockpit. *Just* inside the door.

You are one of the Chosen — and this book falling into your hands was *NO ACCIDENT!* Every word in this book is here because **you** are reading it.

In the hands of "The Others," this would be FORBIDDEN KNOWLEDGE.
But for you, it's what you've always wanted, what you always deserved, what you thought you could never have:

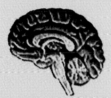

SOMETHING *FOR* NOTHING
It Can All Be Yours

EVERYTHING YOU KNOW *IS* TRUE
"BOB" IS THE PROOF

BEFORE

AFTER

The prudes, prigs, wheezers and weenises, jocks and jerks, pencil-necks and ninnies, super-patriots and fundamentalist fanatics, all think there should be more RELIGION in this country.

Well, have we got a religion for them!!

The Church of the
SubGenius

God's Answer to Fundamentalism
The World's First Industrial Church
"Building a New Heaven and a New Earth — On the Rubble of the Old"

Page ii of *Revelation X:* the "Bob" apocryphon

me in an all-male private school. All I could do was steal *Playboy*s, beat off, and make violent horror movies. I was going to be the next Orson Welles . . . I started doing these really weird art films on money I earned by shoveling dog shit at a kennel. About the age of 16 I switched from being a nice dutiful boy to being a bad hippie.

That sounds like drugs.
Well, yeah . . . I took LSD before I'd ever even tried a beer. A hit of LSD in those days was about 10 times what's called a "hit" today. That's definitely what took me away from the monster movies and into art films with weird sociological statements, AND monsters. Plus, about that time Frank Zappa appeared, and Jimi Hendrix, and the Firesign Theater, and I discovered R. Crumb and underground comix. My main ambition for a time was to be accepted by these guys who do underground comix. That's one of the goals I've achieved, and that part of it was remarkably easy. Making any kind of a living was the hard part. By the time I was 26, I was long-married and struggling in sweatshop film companies editing cheesy business films and being "assistant everything," grip and boom man and best boy, in the dead heat of Texas summer, on low-budget horror features like *Poor White Trash Part II*. But, with Philo Drummond's help, I had written that first SubGenius pamphlet, which, as far as I'm concerned, was

equal to doing *Citizen Kane*. The first place I sent that thing was to the underground comix publishers. The owners threw them out, but two of the artists fished copies out of the trash can—Paul Mavrides at Rip-Off Press and Jay Kinney at Last Gasp.

Those two guys were a big help. They were the first professional artist-types I knew.

I was not actually an outcast in high school. I was a friend to the outcast, the only advocate of the pathetic geeks that everybody else

was shoving head-first into trash cans, but I was in pretty tight with the in-crowd too. Did you ever see that movie by Richard Linklater, *Dazed and Confused*? I could just as well say, "Go see that movie, that was my high school years." As long as you were one of the dopers you were okay. I was like the class beat poet . . . one guy called me "Mr. Natural." I was voted "Weirdest in the Class"—it was something I campaigned for. And this was a school where *every* kid was *really weird*. Most of the other guys I went to high school with, who were going to be these big hippie radicals, all ended up working for their dads . . . I must say that my feeling of achieved vengeance is vast. As a poverty-stricken but infamous *arteest*, I have done things those jocks couldn't imagine in their wildest coked-up dreams. I'll tell you what, though. There's no question that had I gotten laid a little earlier in life, I wouldn't now be working for the Church of the SubGenius. Praise "Bob," it must have been all planned out in advance.

What are the Church's teachings in a nutshell?
Fuck the Normals and get all the Slack you can.

How do you get away with being so weird all the time for so many years?
I have a wife and a color television and they both work. ♦

Tripping to an Odd Universe:
The Mystery of the Codex

Gareth Branwyn

I 've always reveled in stories of shut-in eccentrics who spend their entire lives immersed in some personal inner world: everyone from J. R. R. Tolkein and William Blake to REAL nut cases like New York City's Henry Darger, who spent most of his life writing a 1,900-page epic novel *The Adventures of the Vivian Girls in What Is Known as the Realms of the Unreal or the Glandelinian War Storm or the Glandico-Abiennnian Wars as Caused by the Child Slave Rebellion*. Yes, that's the actual title. The text and accompanying collage illustrations are equally indecipherable. Or how about James Hampton, creator of the tinfoil and light bulb *Throne of the Third Heaven*, now housed in the National Portrait Gallery? His complex, and apparently consistent, spirit-dictated cipher text has never been unraveled.

Little is known of Luigi Serafini, the obviously unhinged imagination behind the *Codex Seraphinianus* (Abbeville Press, 1983). Published in 1981, the *Codex* continues to puzzle and delight those who come into contact with it. A huge coffeetable–size volume, the *Codex* is an encyclopedia and

guidebook to a universe next door that's both similar to our own world and completely alien.

Fastidiously arranged in sections covering botany, zoology, chemistry, physics, engineering, sociology, etc., the *Codex* records a surrealist world where matter is in constant flux, and inanimate objects and organic forms morph from one to the other. A couple making love melt together to become an alligator. A plant grows to full maturity and turns into a fountain pen. The fountain pens are harvested by natives to make jewelry. A plant grows its own rain clouds while a fish peels off a copy of its head and lets it take a fisherman's bait. Nothing is as it appears; things transform into unexpected new forms; anything is possible.

Surrounding the brightly colored pencil drawings of the *Codex* is a cipher text that remains locked. The page and section numbering system throughout the book are consistent and thus hint that the extensive surrounding text may also be meaningful. Thus far, nobody knows for sure. Ultimately it doesn't really matter. The power of the *Codex* is its ability to comfort with familiar ideas and images while totally disorienting one's perception with a shape-shifting world filled with the fantastic, the bizarre, and the macabre. The experience you get from a full descent into the Codex is not unlike a psychotropic drug experience . . . minus the hangover. ◆

SZUKALSKI

GOD-KING EMPEROR OF THE KOOK NATION

by Rev. Ivan Stang

The giant Stanislav Szukalski's footsteps shall reverberate like thunder when his spirit finally strides through the great Fringe Hall of Fame to take his rightful place upon the Throne of the King of all Kook Geniuses.

Like many geniuses, but very few kooks, the late Szukalski displayed the extremes of both—but his genius lay in art, and his kookdom in science, and the two just don't mix. What makes him an astoundingly original artist is also what makes him, as a scientist, possibly the most tragically misguided visionary megalomaniacal crackpot ever . . . the ultimate embittered, misunderstood, defeated, ignored, broke, could-have-been *Savior of the World*. And boy, could he *rant* about it.

Szukalski's work is represented today by only one book still in print, the profusely illustrated *Behold!!!* The Protong. This astonishing oversize tome offers a compressed summary of all mankind's secret history, the truth behind all religions, the forbidden wisdom of the ages, the key to translating every language, and the reason for every human tragedy, all detailed in a raving, floridly vehement style accompanied by hundreds of illustrations of archaeological "evidence," drawn and earth-shatteringly interpreted by Szukalski himself. And this large book is but the most pared-down glimpse into Szukalski's teachings; he wrote and illustrated 39 unpublished volumes on his amazing self-invented all-inclusive one-man science called Zermatism.

Like the best kooks, Szukalski indulges in no false modesty. He repeatedly reminds us that he is the one true genius who has unraveled the secrets of the universe, and everybody else is an intellectual cockroach by comparison. As he humbly puts it, "I have made the greatest discoveries that a human was ever capable of."

But this guy was no sorry little Francis E. Dec–style racist cranking out crappy mimeographed flyers. He really was a genius in a world full of morons. What makes him unique is that no other twisted, demented visionary drew and sculpted this well. Szukalski's graphic style is a truly electrifying blend of the sublimely classical and the grotesquely cartoonish —insanely melodramatic, like Nazi or Red Chinese propaganda posters were they executed by Robert Williams.

Contrasting with the art, Szukalski's writing is a perfect example of the classic, time-honored, frantic top-of-the-lungs FREQUENT ALL-CAPS KOOK STYLE. It's somewhat reminiscent of the great Dr. Bronner of soap bottle fame, or like a terminally sarcastic and

peripatetically enraged Charles Fort— had English been Fort's second language.

Szukalski was born in Poland in 1893, the son of a blacksmith, a prodigy in sculpture who had his first art exhibition at age 14. His family emigrated to America, where the young genius became a rising star among the Chicago intelligentsia, celebrated by the likes of Carl Sandburg, Ben Hecht, and Clarence Darrow. A book of his art was published in 1923. A celebrity (for the time being), he returned to Poland in 1936 hailed as that nation's "greatest living artist." He even had his own museum, but it was destroyed by Nazi bombs . . . and on top of that, he was "betrayed" by the Polish government, which confiscated his remaining sculptures. He fled to Los Angeles, there to become the definitive forgotten, embittered nobody.

However, even though he worked alone, with no academic training whatsoever in any field of science, he toiled on and on with his studies— eventually discovering the actual history of the world, his own version of nuclear physics, how planets are created, and the reasons for all wars and bad people.

His most important discovery (realized from studying such diverse artifacts as Greek vases and Sumerian bas-reliefs) was that throughout history, Yetis or Abominable Snowmen— "Bigfoots" in the New World—have been tainting the pure and noble human stock, producing a half-breed race which today includes all evildoers, politicians, throwback hillbillies, and those with short legs and/or a pug nose. The Pan figures inscribed on Greek vases, for instance, are actually the species of large apes that raped human women.

"The fact that humans have syphilis is due to rapes by these Pans, and all the wart-nosed Greek philosophers, the pot-bellied, waddling pygmoids, were actually descendants of such interspecies bastardy . . . It is of the utmost importance to know that our Human Destiny is afflicted with the greatest calamities (like the two World Wars) because our HUMAN female ancestors were raped by the Apes, the Yetis, the Sasquatches, and our male forefathers copulated with female anthropoids."

One may spot these treacherous Yetinsyny by their longish arms, extended upper lips, undercut noses, and short legs. (All of which, ironically, happen to apply to Szukalski's own physique!) All unattractive people, insecure people, and bullies are Yetinsyny who, because they cannot be loved by a human (being sort of ugly), overcompensate by becoming crazed evil geniuses, ferocious gangsters, rude clerks, or crafty fomenters of bloody revolutions.

Obviously, Szukalski was not fond of the Yeti half-breeds who surrounded him, but he thought there was a place for them; he would have them spew their "animal vitality" in the art world, where they excel. But, he exhorted, if they enter politics, they should be exterminated . . . before they call all misfits together, to be united!

Scorned and ignored by everyone else, Szukalski's theories are granted credence by only one organized group: The Church of the SubGenius. And even then, the orthodox SubGenii believe that Szukalski has everything completely backwards— that, while he was brilliant enough to uncover the great suppressed secret—that interbreeding between humans and Abominable Snowmen had produced all the problems of the world—he was yet deluded enough to think it was the YETI race that was the avaricious, destructive one! (Why is it that even the greatest among us fall prey to self-hatred? For Szukalski himself is the perfect example of the Yetinsyn, that crazed, manic, lusty half-breed between Sasquatch and man. Yet he is blinded to the most painfully obvious conclusion to which his discoveries lead!!)

Before he died (in 1987) I actually got to meet the great man, and, as a representative of the Church of the SubGenius, I posed to him that very question: Could not he himself be the perfect example of a Yetinsyn, and might the Yetinsyny not, after all, be the victims of the evil humans, rather than vice versa?

True to Yetinsyn form, he brushed me off like I was some utter crackpot. ◆

 *Notes*

TOYS AND COOL TOOLS

A toy or a tool is just another lump of matter till you add imagination. The problem with lots of adults is that they let their imaginations shrivel up as they get older. They don't "grow out of" playing with toys as much as they forget how to play with them. Sliding some wooden blocks around on the carpet, pretending they're a choo-choo train, becomes unimaginable and silly. But for Happy Mutants, who are smart enough to keep their childlike wonder alive, toys, and their grown-up equivalent, tools, can be a veritable fountain of youth.

Kids spend most of their time swimming in this mythic liquid. They can breathe life into a plastic doll, turn a cardboard box into a castle, or create an alien planet inside of a sandbox.

But why let kids have all the fun? There are plenty of toys and cool tools that can help us big kids rehydrate our dried-up creative juices. Want to create life? Build a robot that exhibits surprisingly lifelike behavior! Want to be the ruler of an entire planet? Use a computer program to create a new world according to your specifications, seed it with primitive life, and watch it evolve! Want to explore outer space? Join up with other space enthusiasts and build and launch large, suborbital rockets, or talk to amateur satellites from your home computer!

"Toys and Cool Tools" is about the many gadgets and nifty playthings you can use to exercise your imagination, and even includes a peek at *The Eldritch Catalog*, which offers toys from the year 2095! This section also profiles Happy Mutants who've made a living out of playing by creating some of the coolest gizmos around. We hope you'll be inspired to dip your brain into some of this invigorating juice.

As the little kid in *Close Encounters of the Third Kind* says while the aliens climb in through the doggy door: "Toys!" It's a mantra worth repeating, and repeating often. ◆

Carla Sinclair

What a thrill it was to pry a new Superball out of its see-through plastic package and slam it down to the floor. It would wack the ceiling, whip back down to the floor, boomerang off a wall, bounce off the TV set, and eventually disappear into another room. Sometimes the magical little sphere would hit a window,

snapping me out of my delirious rapture just long enough to take it outside.

I was luckier with the windows than the Wham-o folks were who tested the Superball in the mid-sixties. These new product representatives went to Australia with a behemoth Superball, the size of a bowling ball. During an exhibit on an upper floor of a hotel,

the semi-drunken demonstrators began to play with their huge new toy and, in their exulted state of jubilation, bounced the heavy ball down the hallway. Someone meant to catch it at the other end, but missed. The oversize Superball crashed through the window, hit the pavement, took one humongous bounce, and plopped into the back of a

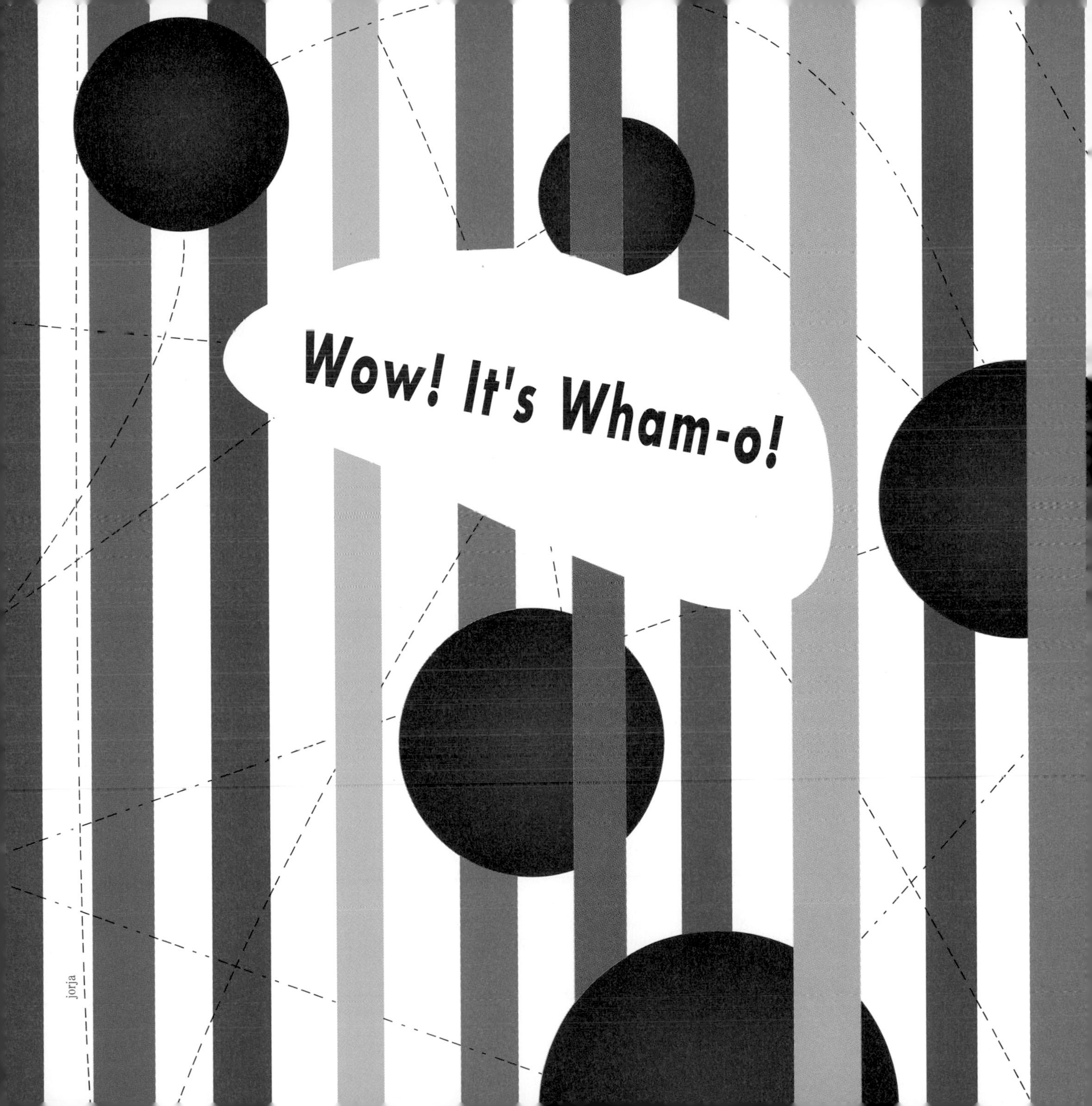
Wow! It's Wham-o!
jorja

convertible. Thus the Superball was introduced.

But the Superball was only following Wham-o's already illustrious reputation for creating extremely basic yet captivating toys. Almost a decade earlier, in 1957, a man named Fred Morrison was throwing his Pluto Platter down a California beach. His combined interests

in flight and a new substance called plastic had inspired him to make his plastic flying disc. When enthusiastic Wham-o owners Rich Knerr and Spud Melin happened to see this man flinging his strange new toy across the sand, they bought the Pluto Platter from Morrison and all three became millionaires. Of course "Pluto

Platter" was changed to "Frisbee," renamed after the Frisbie Baking Company in Bridgeport, Connecticut, whose pie tins were used as flying discs by Ivy League students in the 1920s.

Wham-o had a reputation unlike any other toy manufacturer for being playfully wacky and unofficial, as if having fun is some kind of secret joke that we're all in on together. They rightfully earned this post by being the only large toy company to interact with average people who happened to have a great idea for a toy. Anyone could participate. "There was a time in the sixties when Wham-o was the inventor's friend," reminisces Dan Roddick, Director of Sports Promotion for Mattel (which bought Wham-o), referring to chemist Norman Stingley, who came up with Superball's high-bounce formula. "There was a very aggressive effort to bring in ideas from the outside and give them a run. People thought, 'My goodness, I've got a better idea than that. What should I do with it?' They would send it to Wham-o. Wham-o was thinking at that time, 'Well, we've tapped into the spirit of Americana, so bring it on.' We engendered that kind of thinking in American mentality."

Before Wham-o had a chance to digest the fame and fortune Frisbee was bringing them, they were hit with another huge success—the Hula Hoop. "There was never anything like the Hula Hoop before, that swept through with that kind of unbelievable impact. It was a social phenomenon," says Roddick. The Hula Hoop was born a year after the Frisbee when some Wham-o executives went on vacation in Australia (What is it with that country?!) and noticed school kids exercising with bamboo hoops. The execs saw dollar signs. They ran home and replicated these hoops out of the now cherished plastic, and sold 100 million in the next 2 years. "They were known as the crazy guys with odd but simple products," says Roddick "and they were on a roll."

The Frisbee, Hacky Sack bag, and Hula Hoop are Wham-o's biggest money-makers, but they've had a whole slew of other successful and amazingly neato toys, including Water

Weenie, Slip 'n' Slide, Fun Fountain, and the Bow Master. Wham-o's Silly String ranks at the top of my cool-toy totem pole. Just the electrifying pink of Silly String is enough to overcharge my batteries, not to mention the toxic plastic smell that brings joy to my nose. The rubbery gummy texture of the string that crackles when squished (due to air pockets that form) is an added bonus. And unlike the Frisbee or Hula Hoop, Silly String requires no skill, just an obnoxious index finger to press the squirting button, and a cowering defenseless target.

Although most people think of Frisbee as Wham-o's debut, the toy company actually began in 1948.

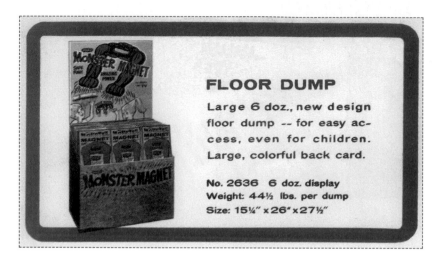

FLOOR DUMP

Large 6 doz., new design floor dump -- for easy access, even for children. Large, colorful back card.

No. 2636 6 doz. display
Weight: 44½ lbs. per dump
Size: 15¼" x 26" x 27½"

Knerr and Melin were high school pals and went to the University of Southern California together. Both men were avid travelers and hunters, so when they finished their studies, they decided to use some family money to create and market a slingshot. They made their toy out of ash wood, and named their start-up company "Wham-o" after the *whammo* sound their new slingshot produced. For the next nine years Knerr and Melin continued to churn out hunting toys and equipment that fit into the world of gaming and fishing, until Frisbee brought them the confidence and capital they needed to do the zanier, more offbeat projects for which they're known.

Of course no company is perfect, and Wham-o has had their share of bloopers. "Instant Fish" was one of their biggest let-downs. Melin had taken a safari to Africa where he learned about some breed of fish that encapsulates itself in the mud during the dry season. Then when the rainy season hits and rehydrates the capsules, the fish break out and go on with their daily routines. "Great!" Melin thought "Just add water—instant fish!" The excited toy-maker packed up some of these fish and sold an incredible million dollars' worth of pre-orders for Instant Fish. Then when he got back to Wham-o's headquarters, they couldn't find the formula to get these fish to breed and encapsulate, so they had to cancel all orders. Instant Fish never got past the prototype box.

Mad Mad Mirror and Nutty Notter were other products that never made it off the Wham-o grounds. Mad Mad Mirror was supposed to be a party game that you would hold up to another person. If you'd squeeze the frame of the mirror you could get a reflection of yourself combined with the features of the person on the other side. The game didn't fly. Perhaps the experience would've been too upsetting for your average party-goer. Nutty Notter was a string with a weighted end that you threw into an overhand knot. The rules seem simple enough, but in test groups, frustrated guinea pigs found the game to be too difficult.

The Cricket House did make it to the toy stores, but didn't stay on the shelves very long. What a surprise! I thought every parent would enjoy the incessant nocturnal chirps and cricket escapees creeping around the house!

Although Melin and Knerr are still playing somewhere on Earth, they sold Wham-o in the early '80s to Kransco, which was resold to Mattel a decade later. Roddick, who began working for Wham-o 20 years ago, says that creating new Wham-o–like products is one of Mattel's big goals, but Roddick isn't ready to disclose what they are just yet. He does predict, however, that the Wham-o spirit will live on. ♦

BUILD A BUDDY OUT OF SCRAP PARTS!

HERE'S HOW!

Gareth Branwyn

One day, after gorging himself on too many Felix the Cat episodes on the ol' electronic baby-sitter, my son Blake turned to me and said: "Dad, can we make a robot?" (He was inspired by an episode where Felix is chased by a killer 'bot.) It was like a scene from Proust. The words "build a robot," being spoken by a six-year-old (in my genes!), were my cake soaked in tea. It instantly transported me back to a moment in my own childhood.

I was also six. I had gotten an Erector Set for Christmas. After seeing the ads on TV and the sets deceptively expanded and posed in magazine ads, I had blown the toy way out of proportion. I thought it could do anything. I was convinced that I was going to be able to build a robot if I got that kit for Christmas. I got a kit all right . . . the very Basic kit. It had one motor, I think, and a fistful of struts, panels, and connectors. I was crushed, but through some kink in my imagination, I refused to believe this wasn't going to build me a robot. The next weekend, I was at my cousin's house. I started telling him about the Erector Set and

my boasts soon spiraled outta control. I told him that not only could I build an actual robot, but that I already had. It could walk, talk, and help me with chores around the house. It was my new sidekick. When he said, "Great! I'll see it next week when we visit your house," I knew I was royally screwed. I spent the week in misery. I futzed and tinkered with that Erector Set, hoping, by some stroke of Pinnochio-like magic, my lifeless little robot would animate. When cousin

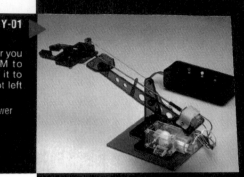

ROBOTIC ARM™ **Y-01**
Wired Control

Using the hand-held wired controller you can direct the ROBOTIC ARM to move small objects. Command it to grab or release, lift or lower, pivot left or right.
- Movement: 3 DC motors provide power to gears and drive shaft
- Control: Wired control box
- Power source: 2-C batteries ✝
- Color: Smoke gray

Leslie came the next weekend, it was the first thing from his lips as he bolted from the Studebaker: "Let's see the robot! Where's the robot?!" When he discovered the truth, he burst out crying and tattled to my parents. It was the first time I remember being really punished for anything. The incident stuck in my craw. Every time I'd see toy robots, things like the Hero kits, and the menagerie of oddball 'bots in *Star Wars*, I'd think about my anemic Erector Set robot.

My son barely had the words out of his mouth and I was already planning what we could do. We started designing right away. My dream robot used realistic '90s technology and was within a budget we could afford. His dream 'bot could transform, had lasers and guided missiles, and was about 9 feet tall.

Over the last year, we've built a number of robot experiments and continue to plan our full-blown answer to C3PO. Our most exciting discovery has been the LEGO Dacta line of computer-controllable building sets. This is the same technology as the regular LEGO building blocks, except they've added gears, sensors, pneumatics, motors, and computer controls. These kits, originally developed for grade school science and technology classes, have a huge following in university robot labs and among robot hobbyists. MIT students have created several tiny microcontroller kits that can be built into your LEGO creations, so that, with an added DC power pack, your 'bots can roam freely. Blake and I have built several of these cute little creatures. One is an "artbot" that can hold color pens and draw its own pictures. The great thing about LEGO-made robots is that they can be easily tinkered with as you learn more or have new ideas. Our next project is going to be building a mobile robot that uses a set of multiple sensors (heat, light, sound, touch) and some basic rules to generate sophisticated behavior. After that, a stair walker is on the drawing board.

I figure, if we take our time and ramp up slowly, by the time Blake is a young teen (if he's still interested), we can tackle our dream 'bot . . . you know the one . . . It can pick up your room, take out the trash, serve drinks at parties, and talk back to your mother. "Son, pass me that 68HC11 chip and that infrared sensor, I've got an idea." ◆

To get started in garage robotics, the two most valuable things you'll need are the LEGO Dacta catalog and the book *Mobile Robots*.

LEGO Dacta

Catalog free from 555 Taylor Road, P.O. Box 1600, Enfield, CT 06083-1600. 800/527-8339. Dacta is the company's educational division offering LEGO Technic kits. Besides the LEGO blocks, there are sensors, motors, switches, lights, gears, pneumatics, and computer control hardware and software. You can buy the components in kits or in separate parts packs. It'll take an investment of at least $100 to get you started. Figure at least another $200 if you want to do some real tinkering and $500 for a serious mini-robot lab.

Mobile Robots: Inspiration to Implementation
Anita M. Flynn and Joseph L. Jones, 1993, 336 pgs.
$39.95, ISBN 1-56881-011-3
A. K. Peters, Ltd., 289 Linden Street, Wellesley, MA 02181. 617/235-2210.
Mobile Robots is the bible of amateur robot builders. It covers everything from basic robot theory to design, construction, operation, and troubleshooting. The book includes semi-detailed plans for two different 'bots. A "Yellow Pages" in the back covers suppliers, products, and tech journals. You need this book. A. K. Peters also sells complete robot kits.

Muscle Wires Project Book
Roger Gilbertson, 1994, 128 pgs.
$17.95, ISBN 1-879896-13-3
Mondo-Tronics, 524 San Anselmo Ave. #107-02, San Anselmo, CA 94960. 415/455-9330.

Email: mondo@holonet.net
Nitinol (pronounced: "night-in-all"), also known as "Shape Memory Alloy" or "BioMetal," is a nickel-titanium wire that contracts like a muscle when electricity is applied. Nitinol is fun to play with and the Muscle Wires Project Book has lots of ideas for cool applications. The last project in the book is a nifty six-legged robot that runs on "muscle" power. Mondo-Tronics also sells Nitinol wire in various diameters and lengths. Blake and I

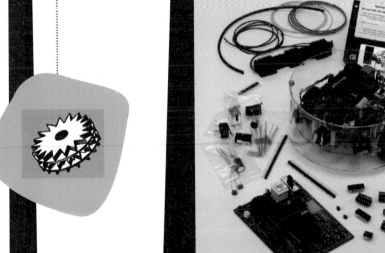

want to experiment with a robotic arm using Nitinol.

The Robot Builder's Bonanza: 99 Inexpensive Robotics Projects
Gordon McComb, 1987, 326 pgs. $17.95, ISBN# 0-8306-2800-2
Tab Books, Blue Ridge Summit, PA 17294-0850.
A classic garage robotics text. Covers many aspects of robotics (base, locomotion, arms, sensors, navigation, and control) and offers a series of experiments using surplus parts, bashed commercial kits, and Radio Shack–available components. Kinda funky around the edges (as are all TAB books),

but useful for gearheads on a budget.

Movit Kits
Catalog free from OWI, Incorp., 1160 Mahalo Place, Compton, CA 90220. 310/638-4732.
These kits are fun to build, but rather boring to operate. We built the Spider walker with an infrared sensor that makes the creature turn when it comes near obstacles. After several nights of excited soldering, building, and troubleshooting, we spent about an hour playing with it

. . . and we never picked it up again. As it moves, it does look very animal-like (more knuckle-dragging chimp than spider). Now it just looks pretty sitting on top of my monitor. But for $80!?

Comp.Robotics
(USENET Newsgroup)
Discussion and resources on robots. Professional, academic, and amateur gearheads all hang out here. If you have USENET news access, check it out.

NAVIUS™   MV-938
Infrared Sensor

Program NAVIUS to turn left, right, pause or go forward. As the white disk rotates, the NAVIUS infrared sensor reads the program (black markings) that you design.

- Movement: 2 wheels driven by 2 DC motors
- Control: Programmable disk
- Power source: 1-9V & 2-AA batteries ÷
- Color: Smoke gray

BUILDING BLOCK BEHAVIOR

The tiny robot with tank treads comes ambling down the hallway. It finds an open door and scoots into the room. Its heat sensors pick something up and the 'bot makes a beeline for the source (a fireplace). It meets an obstacle along the way (a toy), but easily trucks over it. As it's about to get too close to the fire, it turns tail, as if frightened, and darts under the couch. After a few moments in hiding, it appears again and casually motors out of the room. To the observer, this might look like intelligent behavior. In fact, this series of actions is performed by only a few sensors and a microcontroller that prioritizes them. The scheme is called "Subsumption Architecture."

Here, the robot designer defines the robot's actions (using sensors and actuators) in such a way that higher-level behaviors are built upon "core" lower level behaviors, like the skins of an onion. For instance, a robot might have "obstacle avoidance" as a lower-level action and "light-following behavior" as a higher one. The 'bot will approach a light source, but if it senses that an obstacle is in its path, then the lower-level behavior program kicks in and it will stop moving toward the light. By building intelligence systems this way, a rich set of behaviors can arise from a small number of sensors.

Rowdy Robots

David Pescovitz

On a San Francisco pier in July 1994, a crowd of people gathered to watch The Master and The Beetle fight each other to the death. Children laughed as The Master tore The Beetle's skin open and began to eviscerate it. But The Master suddenly ran out of energy. The audience roared with approval as The Beetle went in for the kill.

No, they weren't attending a pit bull contest, or an ultimate fighting tournament. They were at the first annual Robot Wars, an event created by toy designer Marc Thorpe, where contestants were not risking flesh and blood, but silicon and circuit boards.

"The idea for Robot Wars came from an invention gone astray," says the 50-year-old Thorpe, who for 12 years was chief model-maker at George Lucas's Industrial Light and Magic. "I had this idea for a radio-controlled vacuum cleaner. It was fun but it wasn't very effective. So I took the vacuum cleaner off and, just for the heck of it, mounted a battery-powered chain saw on it."

Over 1000 people coughed up $30 to ooh and ahh as 16 radio-controlled robots—created by engineers, artists, and students from Industrial Light and Magic, Maxis software, and even a Fresno, California, high school—sought and destroyed each other in four separate games and three weight categories.

The rules were basic. Robots were forbidden from firing "untethered projectiles" (such as bullets or missiles), or squirting flammable liquids. Other than that, pretty much everything was fair game.

Thorpe thinks Robot Wars could encourage universities to better balance their budgets between athletic programs and engineering. After all, Robot Wars is a sport, albeit an unconventional one. "Many people don't realize they're sports fans," Thorpe says. "Robot Wars appeals to everyone from those with a World Wrestling mentality all the way to computer programmers." ◆

Robot Wars: 415/267-0577 or robotwars@aol.com.

NOT AVAILABLE IN STORES

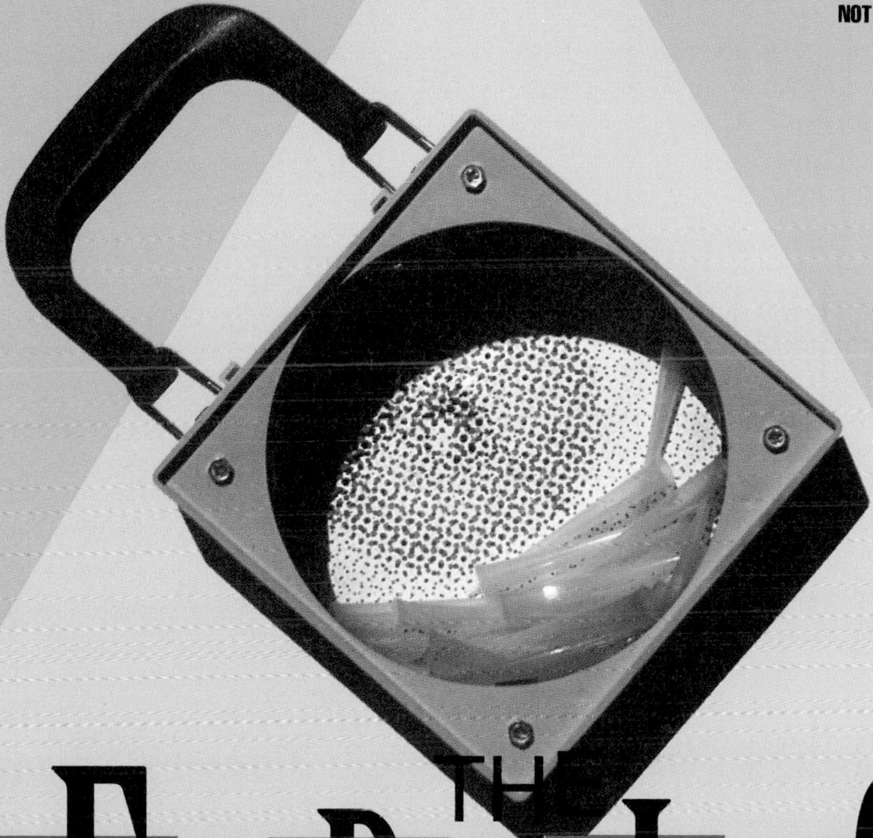

THE ELDRITCH

COMPANY

Creating hard-to-find items since 1322

SPRING CATALOG-2095

©2094

LOVE SPONGES

Spring means love and love means sponges.
4 pack- original and NEW wintergreen.
Surprise someone!

FLAT FOOD PROP

Impress your friends with what you eat.
Preprinted with realistic pizza design!
100% FRESH Paper on card stock.

MEASURING BOX

SHARP-looking box lets you keep time, track
ambient temperature and do simple calculations
all at the same time! Neo-Art-Noveau design.

FEAR ALERT SCENT

Pour these 2 active chemicals around any area and ALL intruders will be stricken with fear! Up to 48 months of security.

HOLY FRAME

Transforms ANY image into a Holy Icon. Don't let the major world religions get the best of you!

PLACE PROFANE IMAGE HERE!

SUBATOMIC SATAN

The world's most famous unpublished book! HARROWING tales of quantum confusion for the general reader. Manuscript only.

THE  COMPANY

Just fill out the enclosed order form and mail. Allow 68 weeks for delivery.

BUILD A ROCKET IN YOUR SPARE TIME!

A tried-and-true Litmus test for nerdiness is seeing how much of a rise you can get out of your subject by saying the word "Estes." Career geeks' eyes will usually light up at the mere mention of this model rocket company from Penrose, Colorado.

Model rockets of the Estes type are still around and the hobby is going strong, with an estimated 1.5 million enthusiasts. Most models are still made from wound paper tubes, balsa wood, white glue, and thin plastic parachutes. The big news in rocketry, however, is that it's grown beyond the bounds of puny models and is on a steep trajectory of bigger and more powerful birds. It seems as though the sky—and beyond—is the limit.

Besides the familiar "model rockets," the other two categories of home-made rockets are "high power" and "amateur" (or "experimental"). High power is similar to model rocketry, with the same basic construction and launch technology, amped up to meet the demands of bigger thrust and higher altitudes. An average high power rocket flight will reach 10 to 15,000 feet. The verified record for a high power launch is 39,000 feet (that's over

7 miles!). High power rocketeers also get more involved in on-board electronics, used for altitude measuring, tracking, photographing or filming the flight, and igniting multiple engine stages late in the flight. This can be a serious and expensive hobby. A nose cone on a model rocket sells for a few bucks, while the nose cone of a high power bird can run over 100 dollars. An Estes model rocket engine costs about a buck and a half, while high power engines can cost hundreds of dollars apiece. The other big difference between model and high power is the regulations put on transporting the engines and flying the rockets. To legally be involved in high power, you need to join the Tripoli Rocketry Association and pass a certification test.

The next step beyond high power is amateur rocketry, where everything is open for hacking. Model and high power rocketry have strict safety rules and forbid homemade engines. Amateurs, while also being safety-conscious, experiment with all aspects of do-it-yourself aerospace. They make their own solid, liquid, and composite engines, and they monkey

around with different construction materials and techniques. The goal of amateur rocketry is to successfully build and fly rockets that push boundaries—in design, propulsion, altitude, etc.

There is still a big gap between high-end amateur rocket tech and low-end commercial and government space technology, but that gap is rapidly closing. It just might turn out that a couple of armchair space geeks, who grew up on the pyro toys from Estes Industries, will end up building an actual spaceship in their garage. Several are currently under construction. ◆

RESOURCES

Estes Industries
1295 H Street,
Penrose, CO 81240
The mother of all rocketry catalogs. Starter sets, kits, motors, tracking devices, and parts.

LOC/Precision
PO Box 221,
Macedonia, OH 44056
216/467-4514
Kits and accessories, ranging from big model rockets to monster high power birds.

Gareth Branwyn

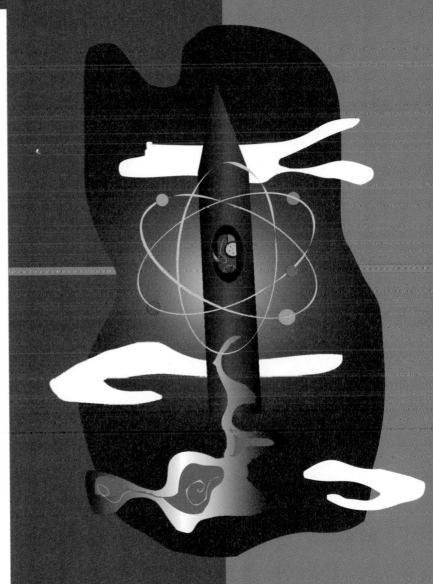

Tripoli Rocketry Association
PO Box 339,
Kenner, LA 70063-0339
The research and advocacy
organization you are required to
join to legally buy high power
motors. Publishers of the excellent
High Power Rocketry magazine.

Pacific Rocket Society
1825 N. Oxnard Blvd., Suite 24,
Oxnard, CA 93030
Internet: ckp@netcom.com
Now building what they hope will
be the first amateur rocket to
carry a payload to the boundary of
space (approx. 50 miles).

Reaction Research Society
PO Box 90306,
Los Angeles, CA 90009
A very well-organized, well-equipped
experimental rocket group. They
own/operate their own launch/test
site in the Mojave Desert. Send for
free brochure.

*Students for the Exploration and
Development of Space (SEDS)*
A national chapter-based student
organization dedicated to promoting
the development of space through
education and hands-on activities.
Internet: http:
//seds.lpl.arizona.edu/seds/seds.html

It's a Schwa World After All

Carla & Mark

Schwa is a line of books, stickers, glow-in-the-dark shirts, buttons, cards, and devices for defending yourself against intergalactic invaders. That's what it looks like at first glance, anyway. Upon further inspection, you'll figure out that Schwa is an art project–cum–fledgling business started by Reno-based artist and commercial package designer Bill Barker. Schwa, explains Barker, is a humorous way to "explore disturbing things such as control, conspiracy, absurdity and despair."

Every Schwa product, from the Xenon Coated Alien Detector, to the Crazy Meter, to the Car Conversion Kit, is illustrated with the same hypnotic, simple shapes of aliens, spacecraft, and stick people. The saucer-shaped ovals in the *Schwa* book (which contains stark black-and-white drawings, unaccompanied by text) represent not only the aliens' spaceships, but also mouths, eyes, TV sets, holes in the ground, etc.

Does Barker believe in space creatures? "I like the strong reactions people have about the idea of aliens. Whether they exist or not doesn't matter; it's the only really exciting myth we have," he says.

To start amassing your own collection of cool Schwa goodies, and save yourself from the imminent invasion, head over to http://www.scs.unr.edu/homepage/rory/schwa/schwa.html on the WWW, or e-mail Barker at schwa@well.com. ♦

$$\partial = MT\, M\pi R_3$$

MUTANT

	PIRANHA	SEA MONKEY	FERRET	IGUANA
Characteristics	A cross between a goldfish and a pitbull; sharp incisors.	Hard to see—must keep in magnified tank; with strong imagination they look just like happy primates.	Long, furry, snouted. Rodentlike, but actually hunts and kills rodents for sport.	Large lizards. Spry when young, lazy as adults. Love to lounge.
Where Can I Get One?	Nearby Amazon riverbanks.	Toys R Us.	Well-stocked pet stores.	Exotic pet shops.
Care/ Responsibilities	High maintenance. Drop body parts into tank; keep fingers at least a foot from the surface of the water.	Mid maintenance. Sprinkle food once a day, scrub sides of tank when monkeys are no longer visible.	Mid maintenance. Feed once a day; when cage kicks up strong stench, clean it.	Mid maintenance. Feed veggies all day long; clean cage 2–4 times/month.
Cool Factor	Contained danger.	The name.	Weird looking.	Dinosaurlike.
Pet Peeve	Owner often gets the nickname "Stubby."	They're brine shrimp!	Highly nervous, stinky.	Sluggish.

David Eggers and David Moodie

PETS

Carla Sinclair

CICADA	A-LIFE	CHIA PET	ROCK
Insect with stout body, wide blunt head, and large transparent wings.	Digital "life forms" you can create on your computer.	Clay pot shaped as cute animal. Embedded with seeds. Sprouts green coat in developed stage.	Comes in many shapes and sizes. Usually hard and shy. Look nice when polished.
Japanese pet stores/trees.	Software stores, the Net.	Walgreens, garage sales.	Backyard.
Low Maintenance. Keep cage stocked with bug chow.	Low maintenance. Be sure computer is plugged in, software installed. Beware of virii.	Low maintenance Water a couple times/week. Set in diffused sunlight.	No maintenance.
Chirps.	Can turn them off.	Corny.	Never dies.
Loud.	Can't hold them.	Corny.	Boring.

Greasy Riders

Kristy O'Rell

Grease. Goopy globs of slimy, slippery fat. The stuff does wonders for frying potatoes, but did you know it's also a helluva way to fuel your car?

Five women cruised a 1984 Grabber Blue Chevy Beauville van from New York to San Francisco last summer on a mixture of kitchen grease and diesel gas, a concoction known as biodiesel. These media artists—Nikki Cousino, Sarah Lewison, Florence Dore, Julie Konop and Gina Todus employed their novice experience in *transesterification* (the chemical process that turns vegetable grease into a usable fuel) to get a taste of the American heartland.

Making their way across the country dressed in cheap orange polyester waitress uniforms, they stopped at greasy spoons to beg the management for fryer fat. They spent hours processing biodiesel in dusty, arid parking lots, meanwhile holding press conferences to provide information about biodiesel and its benefits.

To their surprise, several farmers were already steering John Deere tractors on biodiesel! Receiving a huge amount of positive public feedback, the

photo by Diane Cousine

crew collected over 20 hours of video and audio tape. By the end of the adventure, the women had improved their transesterification skills to the point where they were able to run the van's engine on vegetable oil alone.

What gave these artists the gumption to do such a project? Even four years ago, grease was in these girls' blood. Cousino and Lewison were building a reputation in the San Francisco underground art scene by throwing parties with auspicious themes of waste, excessiveness, and their favorite artistic medium, lard. Then the two women were introduced to upstate New York inventor/environmentalist Louis Winchesky, who had garnered media attention with his ability to convert his Volkswagen Rabbit to run on grease drippings. Intrigued by biodiesel's potential as an alternative to gasoline, Cousino and Lewison (later with Dore, Konop, and Todus) met several researchers, scientists, and ecologists, and discovered that, with the proper tools and knowledge, they could actually pull it off themselves. As Winchesky once remarked, "If you four stupids can do it, anyone can."

BIODIESEL RECIPE WARNINGS AND DISCLAIMERS:

1. We aren't responsible for you. You are responsible for educating yourself about biodiesel as well as understanding this information is quite crude and still in its

exploratative stages. This is public information to be used at your own discretion and risk. Do not use this recipe to make biodiesel, as it lays out only the most basic steps of transesterification. Please contact one of the sources below if you are serious about making biodiesel.

2. We suggest that if you use biodiesel for more than 4 weeks straight you should replace all rubber components of your vehicle's engine with steel or heavy-duty rubber. Or we recommend using a percentage of diesel, at least 20%.

3. Don't mix methanol with your beer. Don't dip your hands in Red Devil Lye like it's Palmolive. These are toxins, people. Remember what Mom and Dad said about the kitchen and bathroom cleaner? We would like to emphasize their remarks with an extra "WATCH OUT!!" Wear good rubber gloves and work in a well-ventilated area. Keep a spare respirator around for safety's sake and work in an area where you have easy accessibility to water and electricity.

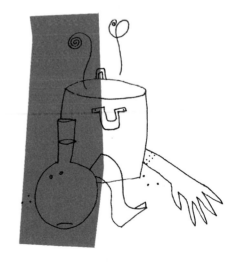

4. LAST BUT NOT LEAST: The utensils, pots, etc. you use should NOT be used for anything but mixing nasty chemicals in your well-ventilated area. Don't drop them in the sink and expect to cook up a casserole and not get really sick.

G.R.

For more information, contact:

Biomass Center: 303/278-0558

Biodiesel Alert Newsletter
American Biofuels Association
1925 N. Lynn St.
Arlington, VA 22209
Phone: 703/522-3392
Fax: 703/522-4193

Biofuels America
Road 1, Box 19
Westerio, NY 12193-9801

Fat of the Land Project
Sarah Lewison
sarahlew@aol.com

BIODIESEL RECIPE

Ingredients:

- Vegetable oil (soybean, canola, preferably monosaturated oils)
- pH paper
- Red Devil Lye (sodium hydroxide)
- Dry gas methanol (MeOH) (You can find it at automotive racing stores.)

1. Take 4 kilograms of used vegetable oil and heat in a stockpot on a hot plate to 120°F.

2. In separate containers SLOWLY MIX 600g (15%) dry gas methanol (MeOH) with 40g (1%) of sodium hydroxide (NaOH) until the sodium hydroxide dissolves. This mixture becomes extremely hot and, on a larger scale, potentially dangerous. A second container should hold your waste oil. Using a drywall mixer bit attached to a 1/2-inch drill, begin mixing the oil, and then slowly pour the dissolved MeOH/NaOH into the vegetable grease. Stir constantly with a wood spoon or a steel rod for 30 minutes.

3. Use a turkey baster to extract a sample of your concoction, and place in a glass test tube (because it is an agitated mixture, you can sample from any portion of the container). Place the test tube in a holder. The glycerin (fatty acids) will sink to the bottom and the methyl esters (biodiesel) will remain on the top. Time how long it takes for the esters to separate from the oil. The faster the separation, the better the fuel. An average time is between 1.5 and 3 minutes.

4. Let the mixture settle for at least 8 hours.

5. The methyl esters should be poured off into a separate, clean container to be washed.

6. Add water to the methyl esters, stirring slightly. Allow the mixture to settle. When the separation looks clean, drain or pump the water out from the bottom and repeat until the water has a neutralized pH level of 6–7 and soap bubbles don't appear. If the methyl esters are cloudy, the mixture will need to be reheated slowly so the water evaporates. White substances forming at the bottom or bubbles forming at the surface are signs of soaps and should be removed or the liquid rewashed.

7. The cleaned methyl esters (the biodiesel) is ready to be poured in the fuel tank of your diesel-powered vehicle.

– HAPPY MOTORING! –

Godzilla's Playhouse

Sarah Borruso

E ver find yourself humming the *Speed Racer* theme song while searching the want ads for a Mach 5? Stop where you are and check yourself into Kimono My House, in Emeryville, California.

According to owner Susan Horn, Kimono My House began in 1980 as a Japanese import store selling kimonos and antiques with "one small shelf" of toys. Today, without a kimono in sight, the tiny shop proudly houses "the largest selection of Japanimation and sci-fi toys in the known universe." An unexpected transformation indeed; toys, robots, and novelties (both new and vintage) have taken over the store's stock, all due to requests from customers who began asking Horn

if she could locate the paraphernalia of their favorite Japanese superheroes. Now the predominantly mail-order business gets requests for the cult goods from around the globe.

Obscurely located on a warehouse rooftop in the Oakland suburb, Kimono My House is *the* place for

truly dedicated fanatics of Japanese sci-fi. Only those willing to call first for directions will ever see this out-of-the-way haven of cosmic toys and robots—but it's definitely worth the trip. A true embodiment of merchandising madness, the store offers a boggling variety of objects featuring favorite characters like Godzilla, Speed Racer, Astroboy, and Ultraman, as well as fringe freaks like Snowgon, Gridman, and Mr. UFO Noodles.

Say you're looking for that perfect gift for the hard-to-please toy robot aficionado; your eye might be attracted

to Mothra. As the robot with a reputation for the most functions, it spits silk, turns right and left, screams, and has a head that moves up and down. Made by Marui, Mothra is a battery-operated, remote-control toy which targets serious collectors at a price of $595. But don't be shy with that silk; a replacement cannister may be purchased separately from Kimono My House for only $9.

Or perhaps you're shopping for a simpler toy, something a little less fearsome. You might be intrigued by an array of products featuring Anpan Man, described by one employee as "the superhero with a head of bread." Anpan Man's nemesis is Viking Man, who is half his size and represents bacteria. Particularly cute and educational, the duo may be purchased together as a windup toy: attached by a thin chain,

"bacteria" trails "bread" incessantly. Made by Toho, these linked adversaries are an affordable $12.

The store's list of unlikely novelties is endless. Maybe you need an Astroboy nail clipper key chain? An Ultraman toilet brush? A pair of Kamen Rider pajamas (adult and child sizes)? Totoro night-light? Cat Bus tissue-box cozy? Godzilla soap dish? Kerokerokeroppi shampoo? Or windup sushi?

Although you probably won't drive home in Speed Racer's Mach 5 (the 1970s "friction-powered" collectible costs $400 even without the original box), you might get some Gummi Godzillas to eat while waiting for the bus to pick you up and take you back to your launchpad. ◆

Kimono My House. Send $2 for mail-order catalog: 1424 62nd Street, Emeryville, CA 94608. phone: 510/654-4627, fax: 510/ 654-4621.

 *Notes*

BRAIN CANDY

It's cheaper than ever to publish zines, videos, albums, and comic books. The power of publishing technology continues to improve month-by-month, and in their eagerness to get the latest and greatest equipment, businesses routinely unload perfectly adequate computers, printers, scanners, copiers, and video and recording gear at garage sale prices. The publications, movies, and albums that do-it-yourself media freaks are producing on shoestring budgets, with a staff of one or two people, are often indistinguishable in quality from the media being churned out by the big boys and girls.

In this section, we'll show you how to express and communicate your artistic urges in the best way possible for the least amount of dough. We'll also introduce you to some of the coolest DIYers out there, and show you how they do it.

The one thing we can't give you is ideas for good content. Science fiction writer Theodore Sturgeon once said that "90 percent of everything is crap." This especially holds true for DIY media. In fact, it's so easy to make a magazine or CD now, that people don't need to have the burning artistic drive (which usually accompanies talent) to jump through all the hoops that used to be involved in getting something published. Sturgeon's law should be revised to say 99 percent of every DIY thing is crap.

Of course, if you insist on publishing lousy art and music, nobody is going to stop you (refer to our section on Supreme Weirdos). But don't expect anybody to read it, watch it, or listen to it. In other words, we'll give you the assembly and shipping instructions, but the contents are up to you. ◆

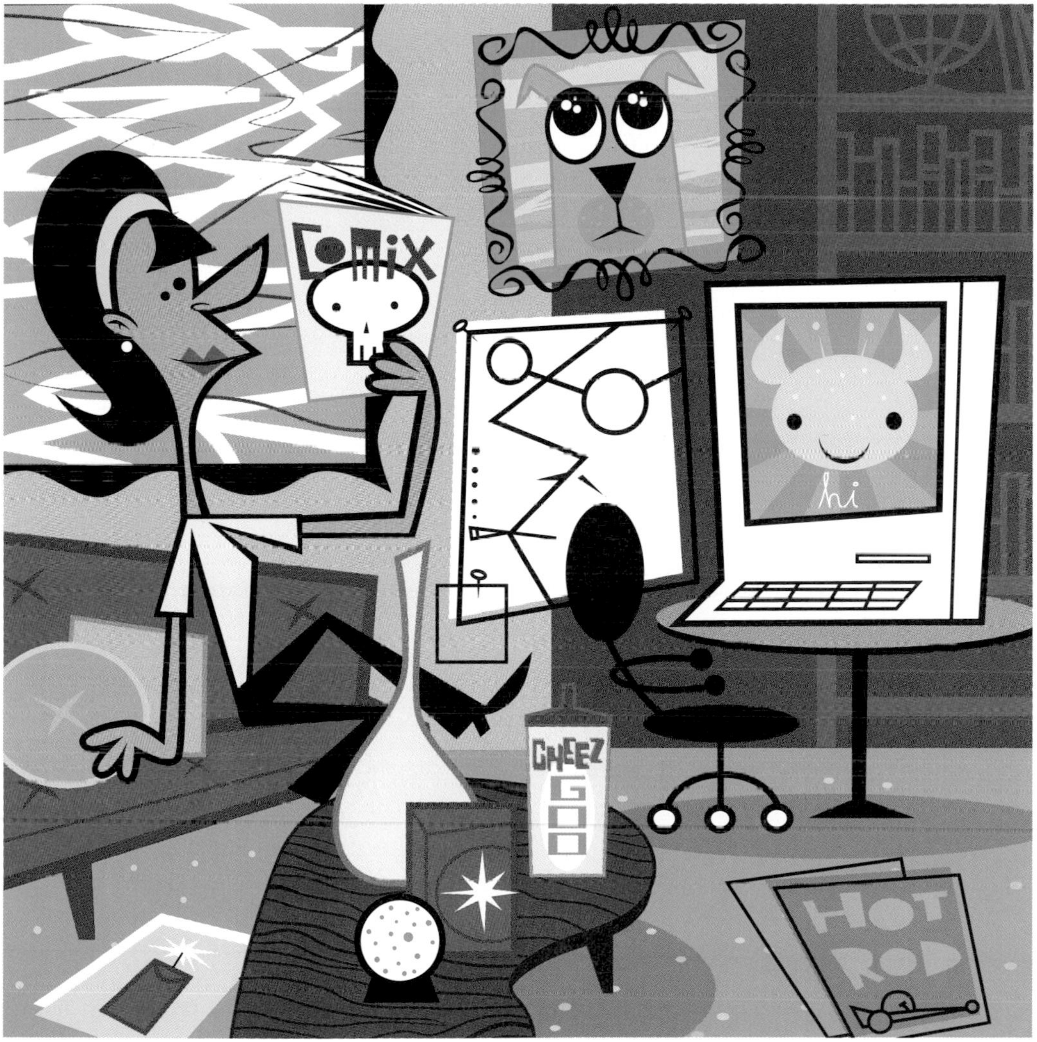

Chip Wass

How to Get

Your Zine

Seen

*"A revolution in technology has inspired
an amazing surge of free expression
and cultural ferment creating the world
of zines: thousands of small publications
which are produced primarily for love
rather than money . . . Most zines start
out with the realization that one need
no longer be merely a passive consumer
of media. Everyone can be a producer!
That's the underlying message of the
zine world, and the greatest thing about
zines. Come join us in this untamed
new world."*
—Mike Gunderloy, *The World of Zines*

I'm not going to waste space
explaining how to make a zine. If
you have an idea, a stapler, and access
to a copy machine, you're in business.
It's so easy, even a creative chimp
could make a zine. Once you show
your brilliant work off to your friends,
however, and they tell you it's the
coolest zine they've ever seen, then
what? How do you get your zine into
the hands of strangers? How can you
get the whole world to appreciate and
idolize you? Just follow this simple

path and soon you'll be one of the masters of the zine universe.

Cover Price

First of all, you need a cover price. Sure, you could give your zine out for free, but unless you have unlimited resources, you'll go broke before getting many issues out. It's usually better to make 'em pay!

Here's the basic formula to figure out how much to charge: cost per copy to produce zine + postage to mail your zine + a buck or two (for unseen expenses and profit's sake) = price of zine. The profit you make should be poured into your next issue if you want your zine to improve in quantity as well as quality.

Now your zine is ready for the unveiling. Look at all the places where your zine can shine!

Newsstands

Yes, your zine can sit on shelves right next to bigwigs like *Spin* and *Wired*. Well, maybe not right next to them, but possibly at the same newsstand.

Most cities also have "alternative" bookstores and newsstands which welcome publications that differ from the mainstream. Whether you want to use distributors or personally deliver your zines to vendors is up to you. Notice the pros and cons of each.

Distributors

I feel a twinge of guilt even bringing up distributors here. They can cause an abundance of stress, false hope, and even bankruptcy. But don't let this scare you! Distributors can also deliver your zine to cities all over the country—even the whole planet— spreading your words and ideas to places you never knew existed. The way to get the most out of distributors while avoiding the cons is to understand a few things before you get involved with them:

1. Distributors usually get a 45 to 60 percent discount off your cover price. If they ask for more, run like hell.
2. Most distributors don't pay until well after you've given them your next issue. It can be a real drag, especially if you're depending on the money to produce the next issue. So plan ahead.
3. Unfortunately, there are distributors (especially the smaller ones) who never pay up. If you get burned once, stop using them! (Prank them if the urge hits.) Call a few times before hating them, however, because a lot of distributors need to be pestered a few times before handing over the loot.
4. Look at the list of distributors (see sidebar, [at end]) who are zine-friendly. This is just a partial list (we can't squeeze all of them on this tiny page) which should help you get on the right track.

Self-Distributing

The obvious advantage to hand delivering your zine to newsstands is you cut out the middle-folk. This means you are in control of where your zine goes and when you get paid. You'll also get a bigger cut of the dough. Self-distributing requires a lot of organization and physical work (like schlepping the things around), but for small-print-run zines it's probably worth it. Your zine will stay pretty local, however, so if reaching super-star status is part of your agenda, this may not be the right route for you.

Note: Frequently visit the local shops that carry your zine and make sure they're prominately displayed. Zines tend to get shuffled to the dark ends of the stands, many times shoved underneath a more popular magazine. If this is the case, grab the whole stack and place them right over another magazine that is at eye-level, center stage.

Advertisements (for free!)

If you're just starting out, advertising for free (yes, free!) is one of the best ways to get the spotlight on your zine. By advertising you'll get orders for your zine through the mail. This means you have no distributors to haggle with and no bookstores taking a cut, just pure profit gushing out of every order. Although there are dozens of ways to advertise, let's just focus on a few of the easiest means for a zine to get attention gratis.

Trading

Swapping ad space with other zines is probably the smartest way to go. Zine readers are always sniffing around for new diversions to stimulate their brains. Just imagine how much drool these readers will produce when they pick up a zine and see your impressive ad displayed. You'll be bombarded with orders. What's more, by trading ads you'll meet other zine owners (make sure you get them to divulge trade tips and secrets), and you'll fill your zine with cool ads (which will make you look real professional-like!).

Internetting

The Internet is used by hundreds of thousands of people every day, and once you're online, it doesn't cost anything to hype your zine all over cyberspace. There are over 5,000 different public forums called USENET groups that cater to almost every interest imaginable. For example, if you have a zine about pranks and hoaxes, post a message on the USENET group called alt.shenanigans telling people how to get your zine. Don't be a dork and overhype yourself, though, because Net dwellers don't like it when their precious world gets commercialized, and they'll flame you to a cinder. Online services such as AOL and the WELL have special interest conferences where you can plug your zine, but you have to pay to use the service.

Guerrilla It!

This is the most fun—and creative—way to advertise. There are googols of things you can do. Decorate dollar bills with your zine's name. Sneak a copy of your zine in a bookstore's window display. Slide your zine into the magazine racks at the dentist's office, the periodical section at the library, and in the pouch on the back of airplane seats. Place your zine in the hands of mannequins at department stores. Anything goes! Soon people will unconsciously think, daydream, and babble about your zine.

Reviews

Think of reviews as another form of free advertising; the only difference is you have no control over what's going to be said about your zine. Since yours is the coolest zine in the world, however, you should send it to as many newspapers and zines as possible (make sure to choose papers who review small publications such as yours). You'll be surprised at the response some reviews will get you!

Factsheet Five

If you only had one stamp to your name, it would behoove you to stick it on your zine and send it in the direction of *Factsheet Five* (Sample $6, PO Box 170099, San Francisco, CA 94117). In each issue, this amazing mega-zine reviews thousands of other zines, free of charge, of course. With FF5's circulation of 13,000 you'll get all sorts of rollicking customers stomping with excitement for your zine.

Other Sources

Here's a few other zines that review zines. Once you start networking with the world of small publishing, you'll find lots of other zine-reviewing zines. This is just a sample to get you started:

- *Ballast Quarterly Review*, 2022 X Ave., Dysart, IA 52224-9667
- *Ben Is Dead*, 6416 W. Olympic, Los Angeles, CA 90048
- *bOING bOING*, 11288 Ventura Blvd #818, Studio City, CA 91604
- *MSRRT*, 4645 Columbus Ave. S, Minneapolis, MN 55407
- *Small Press Review*, PO Box 100, Paradise, CA 95969
- *Zines!*, 221 N Blvd., Richmond, VA 23220-4033

Well, that's it. See? The zine scene isn't so enigmatic after all. No hard-and-fast rules, no important elbows to rub, and no excuses not to join in on the fun. We want to see your zine, so get it out there!

Zine-friendly Distributors
Compiled by the editors of *Factsheet Five*

BLACKLIST Mail-order
475 Valencia St., 2nd Floor
San Francisco, CA 94103-3416
415/255-0388. Completely nonprofit and volunteer-run collective.

CAPITAL CITY DISTRIBUTOR
PO BOX 8156, Madison, MI 53708
608/223-2000. Comics only.

DESERT MOON PERIODICALS
1031 Agua Fria, Santa Fe, NM 87501
505/474-6311. Western U.S. distributor.

FINE PRINT DISTRIBUTORS
6448 Hwy. 290 East, #B-104
Austin, TX 78723-1038
800/874-7082, 512/452-8709
They're a large distributor of all sorts of stuff.

LAST GASP
777 Florida Street
San Francisco, CA 94110
415/824-6636
Sells primarily to comic book stores nationwide.

TOWER BOOKS/MAGAZINES
2601 Del Monte St.
West Sacramento, CA 95691
916/373-2561
Can get zines into all stores.

UBIQUITY
607 Degraw St., Brooklyn, NY 11217
718/875-5491 (Joe Massey)
Distributes primarily to the Northeastern United States.

For the complete list of zine-friendly distributors, make sure to get a copy of *Factsheet Five's Zine Publisher's Resource Guide*. This handy pamphlet lists a lot more zine-coddling distributors, as well as copy shops, desktop publishing centers, and cool bookstores that are happy to carry zines. Send $4 to *Factsheet Five*, PO Box 170099, San Francisco, CA 94117. ♦

The World's Greatest Neurozine!

bOING bOING is the hippest, sassiest, smartest zine in the Universe! It also happens to be run by us, your *HMH* editors. Biased, you say? Never! We actually took the trouble of feeding every zine in existence into a super-computer. In test after test, *bOING bOING* outperformed all other zines.

We couldn't believe it, but computers don't lie! "Brain Candy for Happy Mutants," "A Blueprint for the Flipside of Serious Culture," "Media Culture Brainwash for Now People," and "The World's Greatest Neurozine," are just some of the ever-changing slogans that the supercomputer has generated in struggling to define *bOING bOING*.

In each action-packed issue, we write about stuff that excites us, whether it's a walk on the weird side of Toys R Us, a lesson on how to press your own CDs, or interviews with movie, game, and do-it-yourself media makers. *bOING bOING* also reviews tons of zines, books, music, and toys fresh off the streets of planet Earth. Most importantly, *bOING bOING* tries to stimulate the reader's gray matter, coaxing their pointy little heads into new and abnormal thought patterns.

So what does the name *bOING bOING* mean? Heck, we don't know, but we like to tell people that it represents fun, crazed energy—the kind of energy that bounces from one idea to another, never content to slow down. And *bOING bOING* has certainly lived up to its name—it's hard to pin us down, whether you're talking about geography or content. *bOING bOING*'s had at least 7 or 8 different homes since it began in1989. It's also changed its angle, from a "cyberzine" to its current incarnation as a "pop culture mag for the techno-savvy." We are addicted to movement, seeing it as the catalyst that keeps our brain juices flowing.

Although *bOING bOING* now looks all fancy and gets professionally printed, it began like every other zine, with Carla and Mark sneaking into the offices of Mark's corporate job at night to use the company's copy machine and stapler. We made 100 copies which sold out immediately (thanks to a great review in *Factsheet Five*). Gareth joined the virtual offices of *bOING bOING* (through the WELL BBS) by issue #2, and the three of us have been sharing creative sweat ever since. *bOING bOING* has grown to a circulation of over 20,000, making it the largest zine in the galaxy. A sample issue will set you back $5. Send to 11288 Ventura Blvd #818, Studio City, CA 91604. ♦

G.R.

Ben Is Dead

Catherine Sawall

In the upper echelon of that highfalutin zine scene, Darby Romeo, the founder of *Ben Is Dead* and the ever so popular *I Hate Brenda Newsletter*, is the goddess of pathos, the alternative, and the bizarre. *Ben Is Dead* is her mastermind creation that she started in 1988, after escaping from her suicidal freak boyfriend, Ben. Each issue deals with a different theme and can be anything from raunchy and bizarre to downright useful. One of *BID*'s most recent themes, in the Black Issue (#24), is death. Now death, even in my own little existentialist mind, has always been the scariest of scary topics, so it took a lot of wincing, teeth-grinding, and squirming to get through this one. The weird thing was, I couldn't tear myself away from it.

I was engrossed with the results of *BID* not quite winning a *Sassy* magazine "Reader Produced Issue" contest. They were forced to take revenge. *BID* designed their own, much cooler rendition of *Sassy* (issue #23) instead. It sent me into heady, whirlwind flashbacks of my teen days, with articles about old TV Rockers like that dreamy Rick Springfield. Also added were some smart sex tidbits, which, admittedly, was a nice refresher. Besides, you can't go wrong featuring the sassiest girl around, Chelsea

Clinton, on a glossy pink-and-gold front cover.

Along with zine, music, and comic reviews, *BID* is jam-packed with engaging fiction and relevant reviews. The thing that grips me the most about *BID* is that Darby has this way of ripping her heart open to us, sometimes about Ben and their destructive and uncannily familiar relationship, other times about life's rough edges. Her empathetic and intimate nature pulls you in. Each issue is never under 100 pages, so make sure you have some time on your hands because once you pick it up, you won't be able to put it down. Sample $4, PO Box 3166, Hollywood, CA 90028. ◆

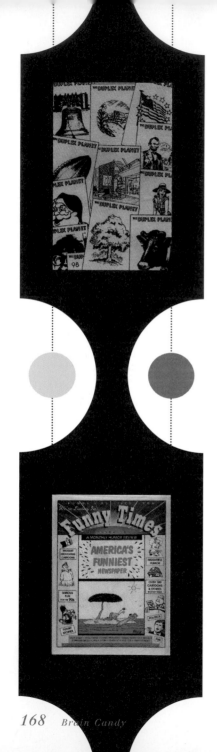

The following is just one-zillionth of the cool zines that we have in the Happy Mutant offices. Read, order, and enjoy! ◆

Factsheet Five

PO Box 170099
San Francisco, CA 94117
Sethf5@well.com
$6/sample issue
$20/6 issues
Factsheet Five reviews thousands of zines as well as music, books, and other cool media. *F5* is a must-have for anyone interested in the zine world. Highly recommended.

Funny Times

PO Box 18530 Dept 2AC
Cleveland Heights, OH 44118
$19/12 monthly issues
The folks at *Funny Times* had the bright idea of making an entire newspaper out of comics and other fun stuff. Each issue is filled with political cartoons, underground comics, humor columns, the always interesting "Harper's Index" and Chuck Shepherd's "News of the Weird."

Duplex Planet

David Greenberger
PO Box 1230
Saratoga Springs, NY 12866
$12/6 issues
Duplex Planet has become one the most successful zines to have emerged from the zine "explosion" of the '80s. The formula is simple: David Greenberger, a former nursing home employee, goes around to various homes asking the residents their opinions on things. The most basic questions can yield odd, funny, and often profound results.

N6

PO Box 1394
Hollywood, CA 90078
n6@cyberden.sf.ca.us
$2/sample
N6 is a high-quality zine with a nice mix of material related to fringe technology.

Nancy's Magazine

PO Box 02108
Columbus, OH 43202
$3/sample
Nancy's Magazine is a very cute zine with uncommon themes like "ground," "power," and "lite," and Nancy manages to make them quite interesting. She sneaks in all sorts of added goodies which make this zine extra fun.

Chip's Closet Cleaner

Chip Rowe c/o *Playboy* Magazine
680 North Lakeshore Drive
Chicago, IL 60611
chip@playboy.com
$3/DOS or MAC disk
Chip digs up all sorts of campy personal relics from his closet and shares them with the world in this wonderfully entertaining digital zine. ◆

Do-It-Yourself Book Publishing

Gareth Branwyn

By now, almost everybody knows what zines are (even if half of them pronounce it "zyne"). MTV, CNN, local papers and TV news shows, and anyone else looking for a human interest story with an edge, have covered this do-it-yourself publishing movement. A new form of publishing has now reached mainstream pop culture acceptance. Self-produced tapes and CDs, while not getting as much press as zine publishing, have also become a legitimate option for musicians seeking an audience without having to wait to be "discovered." What most people don't realize is that, in the realm of book publishing, desktop technology can

Mark Frauenfelder

also get you published long before mainstream publishers take notice. Whether you're looking to publish poetry, artwork, your great American novel, or some obscure technical material with a small audience, on-demand publishing (or sometimes called "Books-On-Demand," or just "BOD") may be the way to go.

To crank out your own on-demand books, you don't need much in the way of technology. If you want to do most or all of the production yourself, you'll need a good desktop publishing (DTP) setup with, ideally, a fast, high-resolution printer, and one of the many home-bindery systems available. That's the more expensive way to go, but it will give you a cheaper per unit cost and complete artistic control over the product. If you don't already have a snazzy DTP system, you can get any part of the process done at a local copy shop. For instance, if you have a good computer and average-speed printer, you can do the original artwork at home and then take it to the copy shop for duplication and bindery. This will raise your per unit cost, but you won't have to invest in a fancy printer and the bindery equipment.

The beauty of on-demand publishing is that you only print as many copies as you need. That way, you save money on the books you don't have to carry in stock. If you get your magnum opus printed and bound at a local conventional printer, it will only make sense to get LOTS of copies done at once. Sure you save money per copy this way, but what happens if you sell only 30 copies of your book and the other 470 copies become a mouse condo in your attic? Then how much money have you saved?

And, before you turn your nose up at the idea of a funky-looking self-bound book, look at some of the work that's been done using this technology. Of course they don't look like a mass market offering, but as in zine publishing, creativity and innovation are key. For instance, if you want a commercial-looking color cover for your book, you can get that done professionally and print the insides yourself. Or you can get color dummy covers that have designs printed on them already, and all you have to do is overprint the cover text on your laser printer. If you want something cheaper than full-color, but still very attractive, there are very fancy laser-compatible papers that you can purchase in small quantities.

Once you've printed and bound your masterpiece, you're gonna want to sell it. Unfortunately, most bookstores will not deal with mom & pop book publishers. The best way to get the word out is through direct mail, zine review pubs like *Factsheet Five* (which also covers books), and specialty pubs that cater to your subject matter. And, while many people use on-demand book publishing to produce vanity books, poetry, and other non- or low-commercial works, you can even go into this type of publishing as a serious business venture. If you have a special skill or some obscure knowledge, you can produce highly specialized volumes that can sell for big bucks. A book on collecting antique fish-tank ornaments that cost you $5 to produce can easily sell for $25 to $50. And yes, my friends, there really are people who collect antique fish-tank ornaments. Who knew?

RESOURCES:

The Complete Guide to Self Publishing
Tom and Marilyn Ross
Writer's Digest Books
1994, 432 pgs., $18.99
A very useful guide to self-publishing and self-distribution. Recently updated to cover electronic publishing rights and other changes in the publishing world. Includes lots of real-world examples.

Synergetics
Box 809
Thatcher, AZ 85552
602/428-4073
Synergetics' owner Don Lancaster is the guru of book-on-demand publishing. Most of his numerous books on hardware hacking, personal computing, and home business are done completely in-house. His *Book-on-Demand Resource Kit* ($39.50) contains do-it-yourself articles, examples, catalogs, software, and other goodies related to DIY book

publishing. If you're serious about producing your own books, Don is a good person to contact.

Paper Direct
100 Plaza Drive
Secaucus, NJ 07094-3606
1-800-A-Papers
This catalog is a gold mine for zine makers, book publishers, and urban absurdists looking to make phony stationery, signage, certificates, and other simulated business materials. For on-demand publishers they sell fancy papers, cover stocks, color dummies, and low-end desktop bindery equipment. The prices are not super-cheap, but they have fast service, lots of cool stuff, and they sell in small quantities.

Unibind
4125 Prospect Drive
Carmichael, CA 95608
916/967-6401
Makers of the Penta-Bind and Pelsaer bindery systems. Highly recommended by Don Lancaster, these hot glue systems are durable, attractive, and

reasonably priced. The Pelsaer system lets you use your own full-wrap custom covers (allowing you to have a conventional lettered spine).

The Underground Guide to Laser Printers
The Editors of *Flash Magazine*, 1993, 162 pgs.
ISBN 1-56609-045-8
$12 from Peachpit Press
2414 Sixth Street, Berkeley, CA 94710
800/283-9444
Flash Magazine
Riddle Pond Rd.,
West Topsham, VT 05086
Fax: 802/439-6463, $15/year (6 issues)
If you're going to use your laser printer as a publishing engine, you're going to want to know more about it and how to keep it maintained and in top working order. *The Underground Guide to Laser Printers* and *Flash Magazine* will bring you up to speed. The book covers the basics on cleaning, maintaining, changing fuser-rollers, and troubleshooting image problems. The magazine offers bimonthly insights of interest to the serious desktop printer. ◆

A Guide to
Mutant Music Makers

Gareth Branwyn and Jessica Wing

Popular music is about reaching the greatest number of people, by *generating* tunes that will *infect* the listener. But what about music that tries to fight the popular drift—music too weird, discordant, and downright goofy to easily paddle into the mainstream? Here's a brief sampling of our favorite medicine for fighting the mainstream music virus.

The Boredoms
The Boredoms are the primary purveyors of "Japanoize." Their irregularly-tempoed, bludgeon-therapy guitars mow down puny American ears like Samurai monster trucks. Their crashing noise and distorted chanting simulate an ongoing, epic cartoon of killer robots plagued by Tourette's syndrome. Some of the Boredoms' popularity is based on their brilliant butoh-meets-slapstick live performances. Their album *Pop Tatari* (tatari: evil incantation, hex) is the *White Album* of Japanoize.

—Jessica

Einstürzende Neubauten
This Berlin-based band (whose name means "Collapsing New Buildings") put art noise on the avant-pop music map. EN mixes rock instruments and standard rock tropes with tools and cast-off junk. Primitive peoples used to make music with the sticks, logs, and rocks around them, why shouldn't (post)industrial-age humans do the same thing? *Strategies Against Architecture I* and *II* (Mute) are decent compilations of the band's work.

—Gareth

Esquivel
Esquivel, the king of lounge music, was an "easy listening" phenomenon in the '50s and '60s. He produced copious amounts of perky instrumentals filled with bongos, xylophone, slide guitars, and a plethora of other exotic instruments. Esquivel is from Mexico, and he peppers his "space-age bachelor pad music" with Latin rhythms,

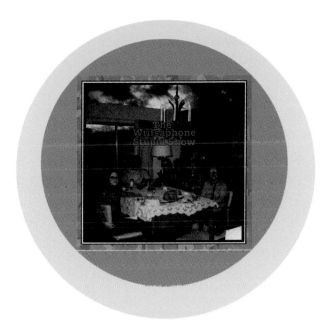

horns-a-plenty, and South-of-the-border suaveness. A compilation of Esquivel's music has recently been reissued on CD. *—Jessica*

Frith, Fred

Avant-troubadour, guitarist/multi-instrumentalist, and British expatriate, Fred Frith has been traveling the world for the last few decades, playing with musicians such as the Residents, Tom Cora, John Zorn, Material, and others. He was a member of the seriously weird '70s art-damage bands Henry Cow and the Art Bears, as well as Skeleton Crew and Naked City in the '80s and '90s. Skeleton Crew's delightful *Learn to Talk* is recommended. *—Will Kreth*

King Missile

The first time I heard "Jesus Was Way Cool," my high school alienation, residual silliness, and religious apathy all imploded in one magical moment. I listened to it over and over, reciting it like a mantra: "Jesus was way cool. He told people to eat his body and drink his blood. That's SO cool." Like this one, many of King Missile's songs are hilariously funny monologues, either sung or spoken, over appropriate background music. Get *Mystical Shit*. *—Jessica*

Kraftwerk

Another band that worked wonders with slicked-back hair, tight uniforms, vacant mannequin stances, and cold electronics.

Surprising, for a band that tried to leach all the soul out of rock and roll, they proved to be a big influence on the funk movement, and subsequently, rap (not to mention "new wave," "techno," and other obvious genres). Their samples are everywhere. *—Gareth*

Negativland

Beyond all the celebrated "fair use" lawsuits and "the U2 incident," the real story behind Mark Hossler and the gang is that they were the unwitting victims of a classified U.S. Government mind control experiment in their native Contra Costa, CA, county. "The DOME"—as it's called (the very inspiration for the name Negativland) is a

high-frequency subliminal eugenics message that tells teenagers to drive muscle cars, breed, shop, and watch round-the-clock TV. Negativland's antidote has been audio "culture jamming," the now popular term that they originated. Check out *Escape from Noise* on SST Records.   —*Will*

Partch, Harry
Born in Oakland, CA, in 1901, Harry Partch was a self-taught musician, composer, instrument inventor and maker. Not content with anything conventional, he invented not only an entire orchestra of instruments, but also a new system of intonation for them. His instruments had exotic names liked "Spoils of War," "Cloud Chamber," and "Chromelodeon," and were made out of recycled glass bottles, military shell casings, junk, and hacked conventional instruments. Works include *2 Settings for Finnegans Wake* and *And on the 7th Day Petals Fell in Petaluma*.   —*Gareth*

The Residents
The Residents' uncompromising weirdness and pioneering efforts in performance art and music videos have made them one of the most influential avant-pop bands. From their early *Meet the Residents* and *The Third Reich and Roll* albums of the '70s to their *Mole* series in the '80s, these masked men from Louisiana continued to make music that defied description and was always laced with deliciously strange humor and impressive musical ideas. With the release of *Freak Show*, their best-selling CD-ROM, the Residents seem to have a watchful eye on the future.   —*Gareth*

Shatner, William
Bill Shatner's attempted break from the *Star Trek* universe into the recording business was one of the most ill-conceived ventures *ever*. His hyperbolic, hyperactive spoken-word versions of rock classics are hysterical, and painful—like watching your dad try to dance to Prince.   —*Jessica*

They Might Be Giants

The two Johns (Flansburgh and Linnel) who make up TMBG combine impressive, almost effortless, musicianship with a warped compositional sense and a bizarre range of subject matter. They sing odes to statues, charismatic dirt bikes, palindromes, girls who ignore them, and the Milky Way. Recommended albums: All of them! You can also call their song-a-day message machine at 718/387-6962. —*Gareth*

Waits, Tom

Who is Tom Waits really? Is he still the seedy LA piano bar player/ Bukowski-esque singer-songwriter of the '70s? Is he the bullhorn toting, ersatz carny barker of the '80s *Frank* album trilogy? Or is he the dignified Sonoma County, CA, resident (only occasionally spotted drunk at S.F.'s City Lights books) interpreting Kurt Weill for the kids? Recommended disc: Swordfishtrombones (Island Records). —*Will*

Ween

Ween is two slackers who can kinda play guitar, at least good enough to make several albums' worth of inspired weirdness. There is an unidentifiable familiarity to the music of these boys from New Hope, PA, like a melted together version of your parents' and your lame older brother's record collections played at the bottom of a fish tank. I recommend *The Pod* and a big bong hit. —*Jessica*

Zorn, John

Agent provocateur or loudmouth bullshit artist? Composer/ saxophonist John Zorn keeps the critics guessing. Known for his car alarmesque alto sax playing, polymorphous genre dipping, and aggro world view, Zorn is certainly an American original. Today, he's more direct with his own playing than he was in his 1980s deconstruction phase. A lover of cartoon, spaghetti western, and TV spy show themes, Zorn both reinterprets the past and invents the future. Take a trip to *Naked City*. —*Will* ♦

Mutant Food

Nathan Shedroff and Carla Sinclair

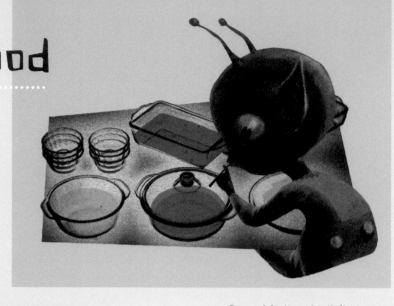

GREEN GLOB GAME

Green tea ice-cream and wasabi (sushi's horseradish) are similarly weird, moldable, and the same shade of green, which make them perfect candidates for this party game: One person sits with a scoop of wasabi, the other with a scoop of ice cream—nobody in the party knows which scoop is which. The two players each take a bite of their "dessert" and act like it's yummy, even though one player has a mouth full of fire. The rest of the party has to guess who really got stuck with the green inferno. Those who guess wrong must take a swig of sake.

MUTANT MEAL CONTRAPTIONS:

Martini glasses
Crazy straws
Swizzle sticks
Jell-O mold
TV tray
Plastic ice cubes
Ornate plastic toothpicks
Absinthe strainer
Pez dispensers
Chemistry set glassware

FAVORITE FUN FOODS:

* *Wonderbread Sushi Recipe* (from Rachel in Seattle)—Snip off crusts of thin-sliced Wonderbread and roll flat. Spread fillings of your choice, leaving a border. (Filling examples: peanut butter and banana; Spam; Cheez Whiz and luncheon meat, etc.) Now roll bread into Ho-Ho shape and slice into 3/4" sections. Voilà!

* *Jell-O*—Pure alchemy! From bright and colorful unassuming powder to wiggly, jiggly ecstasy. You can use just about anything for a mold—auto parts or condoms (non-lubricated), for example. Then find some fancy (and tasty) fillings and pack 'em in!

Top 5 Jellicious Mold Fillings:

5. Broken pretzels and potato chips
4. Canned fruit cocktail (heavy syrup)
3. Sugary breakfast cereals
2. Tequila (in lemon Jell-O—salt optional)
1. Pomegranate seeds

* *Wormz & Dirt*—Gummi worms burrowed into crushed Oreo-type of cookies. Ew! Gross me out!

* *Astronaut Foods*—Tang, dried ice cream, aerosol cheese, and dehydrated victuals.

* *Skeleteen Beverages*—Soda-type drinks with weirdo ingredients like ginkgo leaf, skullcap, ginger, ginseng, mad dog weed, and good ol' caffeine. Some of their concoctions include "Brainwash," "Love Potion 69," "DOA," and "Black Lemonade." Call 213/721-3320 to get a swallow. ◆

G.R.

Review My Album, Win a Car!

Will Kreth

The music industry is not known for being kind. It doesn't really matter if you're gifted or enormously talented. It's a hard-assed business where incompetence is often rewarded with a promotion to upper management. In 1979, this ugly truth was dawning on Steve Tibbetts, who was then an aspiring guitarist and multi-track home recording freak from Minneapolis/St. Paul. Rejected by dozens of labels as having the dreaded "no commercial potential" stigma, Tibbetts was undaunted. Showing great verve and cheekiness, Tibbetts compiled all of the rejection letters into a new press kit entitled "Critics Rave!!" This caught the eye of another recording tweakster—a German man by the name of Manfred Eicher of ECM records. Tibbetts was signed to ECM in 1980.

ECM was recently bought by the giant German media conglomerate Bertelsmann (or BMG), and the record label's marketing department had a hard time figuring out how to promote Tibbetts's latest album, *The Fall of Us All*. Realizing how the hype machine works, and also how it *could* work, Tibbetts seized upon the opportunity to somehow finagle a copy of the press contact/media database from BMG and, with his own computer, launch his own guerrilla marketing salvos.

As the former music editor for *Wired*, I was contacted by Tibbetts via a package that appeared in my mailbox. It contained a zine-like collection of newspaper stories from around the world consisting of hilarious feats of human stupidity. Also included was a form letter that was like a Publishers Clearing House sweepstakes notification!

"Review my album *WILL KRETH*—and you may win my CAR! A 1981 Chevrolet Chevette! ! !"

I found out later I wasn't the only writer who enjoyed this kind of flack. Was all this effort successful? Well, from observing the major music magazines, it seemed to work. Positive reviews started appearing in the months following (including *Wired*), and I even received a letter from Tibbetts postmarked Kathmandu, Nepal— thanking me for my review. As an artist, Tibbetts's music stands by itself. As a creative do-it-yourself direct marketer of his own work, Tibbetts has proven that the "mindless juggernaut" of the music industry can be, and should be, hacked. ◆

THANKS, BUT I ALREADY HAVE ONE, STEVE TIBBETTS!

APRIL 1994

CD REVIEW

STEVE TIBBETTS
The Fall of Us All

ECM 78118-21527-2 • 1994, 59:12

Performance ★ ★ ★ ★ ★
Sound Quality ★ ★ ★ ★ ★

Whether it's the electric guitar brain-melt of 1987's *Exploded View* or the more open acoustic guitar designs of *Big Map Idea*, Steve Tibbetts always plays with intensity. He rips your face off with electric guitars that bend and slur like a Dali painting projected onto funhouse mirrors and approaches the acoustic guitar as if he's strumming the spokes of a warped bicycle wheel. Skewed, Derek Bailey-style picking alternates with a folklike melodicism.

The Fall of Us All doesn't extend the Tibbetts paradigm. Most of his music is still based around loops of one sort or another: usually either samples and tapes or soulmate Marc Anderson's percussion. Anderson's pan-global tribal rhythms shift and shimmy like an erotic dancer lost in Africa.

Roll Your Own CDs, Tapes, and, er . . . LPs

Gareth Branwyn

If you're a musician and you've been waiting to "be discovered," forget it! Chances are, you're sucking up to record execs and other industry weasels for nothing. Too many interesting artists spend their creative lives trying to shop their talent to others, when they should be getting on with the business of making music (or noise art, or spoken word, or whatever) and getting it heard. The technology to create, record, duplicate, and distribute has been street level for years now. And it all just keeps getting faster, cheaper, better.

Wanna be a rock 'n' roll star or a badass rapper? Grab yourself some cheesy instruments and an old 4-track, get your noise on tape, send it to one of the fast food stores of CD duplication (see below), and then distribute your shiny silver disks through appropriate zines, over the Net, and other free (or supercheap) venues. What used to cost tens of thousands of dollars (and was therefore out of the reach of the average riot grrrl) is now doable for chump change. I know musicians who have been quite successful doing their own recording, duping, and direct sales, all for under $2,000. Some of them have gone on to larger labels, while others have decided to go it alone for good. Sure it takes a lot of self-promotion and sweat equity, but if you talk to those who are traveling this route, many of them will tell you it's totally worth it. While it takes more time to go the do-it-yourself route, it's certainly the only option for those of us who can't stand working in situations where we're not in control and where the "bottom line" is everything.

Here are some key resources that can help get you started in DIY music making:

DUPLICATION
Disc Makers
1328 North Fourth St., Philadelphia, PA 19122. 800/468-9353.
Free catalog and useful booklets. These guys are at the top of the heap for cheap CD and tape duplication. They're a one-stop shop that does everything from artwork to final packaging and promotional consulting. If you're in a hurry or are not artistically inclined, they will do a pretty good job of designing the covers, inserts, etc. The bummer is, if you do your own artwork, you don't save any money. They feature good CD/tape combo deals with varying production times, levels of art quality (2-color, full-color), and different qualities of tape. Disc Makers also offers a series of useful booklets about independent music production. Ask for (besides their catalog) "Guide to Master Tape Preparation," "Guide to Independent Music Publicity," and the "Directory of Independent Music Distributors." They're all free.

A+R Record & Tape Mfg.
902 N. Industrial Blvd.,
Dallas, TX 75207. 800/527-DISC.
Free price sheets and brochure.
These are the first people that I
dealt with. They did a lot of the
independent punk records in the '80s.
Punk and gospel choirs have been
their bread and butter. They still do
vinyl in small or large quantities as
well as tapes and CDs. This is the
place to go if you're doing your own
artwork and you aren't super-picky
about the sound quality. I did several
spoken art projects through them
and was entirely happy with the
results.

Nimbus Manufacturing
SR Guildford Farm, Ruckersville,
VA 22968. 800/782-0778.
Free CD-Audio and CD-ROM
catalogs. Nimbus does a bunch of
the duplication for larger independents
and bigger record companies. Look
on the inner band on some of your
CDs and you're likely to see their
name. They're known for high
quality and a good long-standing
reputation in the industry. Their
prices are higher than either A+R
or Disc Makers and they charge
separately for graphic services. If
you're a snob about audio quality
and willing to pay the price,
Nimbus is your duplicator. They
also do CD-ROM pressing.

PROMOTION
Once you have your grunts and groans
on disk, you'll want everyone to have a
listen. By far, the cheapest way to get
the word out is through print zines,
e-zines, and appropriate online sites.
Find out which zines would be appropriate by getting an issue of *Factsheet
Five* and ordering a bunch of the music
zines. Each of these will lead you to
dozens of others. Besides getting
reviewed in these publications,
advertising is usually dirt cheap, free,
or on an exchange basis. On the Internet,
there are numerous music-related
discussion groups and World Wide Web
sites that cater to independent music.
The best of these are:

Internet Underground Music Archive
URL: http://sunsite.unc.edu/ianc/
index.html
The IUMA offers online exposure to
independent bands via the World Wide
Web. You can get your bio, promo
materials, and digital audio excerpts of
your work into the archive, all for free.
There are also articles on legal issues
surrounding DIY/indie music and music
on the Internet. This is a popular spot
on the Net for fans of indie music, so it's
a great place to have your work appear.

Kaleidospace
URL: http://kspace.com/
Kaleidospace is another Website devoted
to the promotion and distribution of

independent musicians, along with
artists, performers, CD-ROM makers,
animators, and others. Artists pay a
flat rental fee to showcase their work.
Internet users can order from the
artists online, or by phone, fax, e-mail,
and snail mail. They also offer Gopher
(gopher.kspace.com) and FTP
(ftp.kspace.com) access.

Poke around on the Net and you'll
find countless other places to talk
about your work and how people can
get ahold of it.

CD-ROM & CD AUDIO + CD-ROM
Many of the companies that offer
CD-Audio also offer CD-ROM. The latest
thing is to include CD-ROM data on an
audio CD. The ROM information is
contained on track 1. If the listener
doesn't have a CD-ROM drive, they
just skip that track. This is a great,
not too expensive, way of getting into
multimedia art and music. For more
information on CD-ROM contact:

One-Off CD Shop
800/387-1633 (to find the One-Off Shop
closest to you).

Disc Manufacturing, Inc.
800/433-DISC.

USENET newsgroups
alt.cd-rom, comp.publish.cdrom.
hardware, comp.publish.cdrom.software,
comp.publish.cdrom.multimedia. ◆

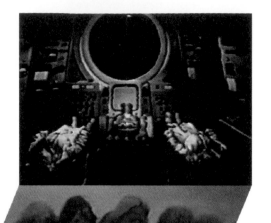

Jamming
the Image
with
Mixmaster
Corman

Richard Kadrey

Hip-hop culture is scavenger culture. Don't have a band? Don't have a bassline? Sample it. Scratch it. Slice and dice it. Pluck something from the air, toss it into the brew, and mix it into something never heard before.

Older than hip-hop is Carnival culture, a universe based on sleight-of-hand, combining the grotesque (freak show superstars such as the bearded lady and the eternally bleeding man), with the beautiful (nymphets in see-through togas posing in faux-Roman ruins for "art" photographers). It's a world that's crude and loud and glitters like cheap industrial diamonds—impossibly and unnaturally bright.

In the '90s, mix-and-match art is as common as nose rings and tribal tattoos. Media pillagers from Afrika Bambaataa to BLK Lion, from Negativland to Emergency Broadcast Network, have constructed a whole aesthetic based on ransacked pop culture. Ahead of them all, though, is Roger Corman, with his splicer under one arm, reels of Soviet techno-fantasies under the other, and a grifter's toothy smile plastered on his mug.

Corman is the granddaddy of Carny hip-hop. In the late '60s this renowned cheapskate and hustler extraordinaire combined Carny hustle with a hip-hop sensibility into a series of weirdly compelling American Dumpster culture sci-fi spectacles.

His first experiment is probably the least successful of the bunch. *Battle Beyond the Sun*, released in '63, is really the Russian science fiction flick *Nebo Zowet* with new dialog and a grafted-on rubber-monster fight scene. The retooling of the Russian footage was handled by a young film school troublemaker named Francis Ford Coppola.

Corman next did a chop shop number on the effects-heavy, but relentlessly dull, *Planeta Bur*. This slice of Russian pop science is about the exploration of Venus by a plucky band of brave scientists accompanied by their huge—and hilariously unwieldy—robot, John. Corman handed the footage to Director Curtis Harrington and told him to make the interplanetary snore-fest into something Americans could watch without slipping into a coma. Harrington wrote new dialog, trimmed the running time, and rearranged scenes, and Corman

released it as *Voyage to the Prehistoric Planet* in '65.

The killer of the bunch, though, is the '68 reworking of *Planeta Bur* as *Voyage to the Planet of Prehistoric Women*. This time Corman handed the project to bespectacled geek Peter Bogdanovich. Bogdanovich spliced the original Russian spaceman footage with his new footage of nearly identical women in hip-huggers and big blond wigs. The blondes were the telepathic inhabitants of Venus. They never meet with the astronauts, but watch them from a distance (this way, Corman didn't have to pay for space suits). *Voyage to the Planet of Prehistoric Women* is a surreal masterpiece, obviously two different movies grafted together, but holding enough genetic information in common that they don't reject each other. Each can communicate and riff off its twin in surprising ways. The pterodactyl that was just a throwaway menace in the first two versions is recast as a god-king to the aquatic space babes. The robot John, a walking Frigidaire who weighs down the first two movies, becomes their new deity after the pterodactyl gets iced. And the blondes themselves are a vision, lithe and sensuous in their tight hip-huggers and seashell bikini tops, while the

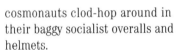

cosmonauts clod-hop around in their baggy socialist overalls and helmets.

You won't find these movies on the shelves of your local Blockbuster. *Planeta Bur*, *Voyage to the Prehistoric Planet*, and *Voyage to the Planet of Prehistoric Women* are all available on VHS or Beta, $19 each postpaid from Sinister Cinema, PO Box 4369, Medford, CT 97501-0168, 503/773-6860. *Battle Beyond the Sun* is available on VHS for $23 (WA residents add sales tax; Canada/Mexico $25, overseas $27) postpaid from Something Weird Video, PO Box 33664, Seattle, WA 98155; 206/361-3759. ♦

MACK WHITE:
A HOWDY DOODY KIND OF GUY

Carla Sinclair

"I still get that magical feeling when I see photos of Howdy Doody or watch old videotapes. I can't explain it. Sometimes I get that Howdy Doody feeling just by eating Hostess Sno-balls," says cartoonist Mack White about his childhood idol. "When Howdy would appear, it was like an epiphany. He was a demigod to me."

Influenced by Howdy Doody, Salvador Dalí, The Three Stooges, William S. Burroughs, and ancient mythology, White's work smacks of the weird and grotesque. He combines '50s and '60s television culture with preternatural and religious monstrosity, ending up with comic stories like "Bison Bill's Weird West Show," where Godzilla-like dinosaur eats clown, dinosaur vomits clown, Indian gives life back to clown, clown is now unfortunate blob of body parts and dripping juice who stars in circus freak show. Among the mutants, snake handlers, perverted puppets, naked nuns, and wacked-out clowns that run rampant through White's work,

Jokey happens to be his—as well as our—favorite character.

"He is my Divine Child," White says about the playfully mischievous bulb-headed multiclops. Jokey was the name of White's first cartoon, a *Li'l Abner* rip-off which he created when he was six years old. Although the present Jokey has nothing to do with its predecessor, White feels a special fatherly attachment to this character.

If you're trying to figure out Jokey's language, you're out of luck. "It's dream language, which cannot be translated," White explains. "Jokey lives in an archetypal place which I've glimpsed in dreams. Each time I do a Jokey strip I discover something new about the place. With this latest strip, I've discovered that Jokey's planet is the home of ancient astronauts who later settled Assyria on our planet."

You'll find White's delightful dementia in his own *The Mutant Book of the Dead* (Starhead Comix) and *Villa of the Mysteries* (Fantagraphics). He's also been featured in *bOING bOING*, *Heavy Metal*, and *Real Stuff*, among other publications. Mack White lives in Austin, Texas, with his wife, Carla. ◆

The Mutant Book of the Dead: $3.50, Starhead Comix, PO Box 30044, Seattle, WA 98103.

Dana Norman

© '94 Mack White

Chris Ware:

The Cartoonist

That Ate My

Brain

Mark Frauenfelder

THE ACME NOVELTY LIBRARY.

Learn to Dance.

You can learn all the steps -- the latest
modern moves. The Boogie Shake.
The Hip Pulse. The Crotch Polish.
New chart method makes dancing
as simple as A-B-C. No appreciation
of music required. Get laid fast.
Don't be a wallflower -- be a Solid Gold
Love Pump. Learn to dance. All based on one secret:
don't think about your life ten years from now.
Franklin Publications. 800 North Clark St. Chicago.

Cartoonist Chris Ware's *Acme Book Dispenser* sits on a table at Chicago's Ten in One gallery. Inside the wood-and-glass machine is a stack of handmade books. In order to buy a book, you must deposit one of your housekeys in the slot. Pull the handle and a book drops through the chute. Your key disappears into a locked box.

Ware's comic book, *ACME Novelty Library*, is kind of like this vending machine, only instead of relinquishing one of your keys, you have to give up a piece of your sanity to get through it.

The first time I read *ACME Novelty Library*, my brain rebooted. The art is incredibly pristine, as if it were drawn by an Asimovian art-deco robot, fed an info-diet of old comic book advertising illustrations. The stories are surrealistic nightmares that touch the ground only long enough to trick you into thinking they make some kind of normal sense, before taking off again for the far side of the psyche. Give your brain a dose of Ware and tear for only $4.50 postpaid from: Fantagraphics, 7563 Lake City Way North East, Seattle, WA 98115. ◆

ariel

BORDEAUX

Ariel Bordeaux is the queen of autobiographical comix. Whether she's talking about her very first kiss, how she hates bra-shopping, or her hellish roommates, she candidly divulges all in her very own hand-made *Deep Girl*. Nothing's ever too private for Bordeaux.

It's fun to be a voyeur! Go ahead and try it! Order *Deep Girl* by sending $2 to: Ariel Bordeaux, 573 Scott St. #L, San Francisco, CA 94117. And here's a sample —*Carla* ♦

THE MELANCHOLY MISSION

BY ARIEL BORDEAUX ©1994

Shopping in the Mission district of San Francisco one sunny Monday afternoon...

I've been here an hour already, maybe more. I knew from the start there was nothing here I wanted.

"rave pants"

Yet, I refuse to leave without purchasing something... it's become an obsession... Why is it so important to me? My hands have become thick with a richly textured filth.

I kinda like this plush toy... but it would just collect dust balls in my over-crowded room... I don't need it.

It seems like everytime I go shopping at places like this I become melancholy... Perhaps I'm fooling myself. I came down here to find just the trinket to cheer me up... but deep in my heart I know that there are more serious matters to attend to...

INK · TEETH · WORRY · HOW TO OVERCOME INSECURITY · BRAIN

Oh well ... I'll look at records...

ALL RECORDS $1.00 · Candyland · jim nabors

It's hard to tell ... could go either way.

yeah..."Maneater" that was a good song...

"vestid de blanco" Carlos Guzman · ALL RE $1.00

This one's sort of beautiful... It's scratched to shit... but I could just hang it up somewhere... Nah... I guess I'll just go now...

So much for my big day at the thrift stores...

Thank you.

Thanks.

I'm glad I came down here, though... It's worth it just to soak in the "imagery"... Rotting neon signs... Screeching children in rediculously frilly outfits... dusty Virgin Mary figurines in all the windows...

LIBRERIA CRIST

3126

God... it's funny... there's so many stores down here that I haven't been in yet, even though they entice me each time. I guess I'm kinda nervous... dumb as it is...

I have this unconscious dread of feeling the awkwardness that comes with my white skin ... although for the most part it's a self-inflicted discomfort, and I usually refuse to engage in the "white-guilt" ... but... I dunno... I can't help but feel that "otherness" when I'm the minority.

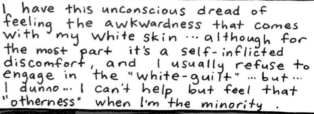

PANCHITAS MEXICAN-SALVADORIAN RESTAURANT No 2

It bothers me that practically the only "cross-cultural" experiences I have are times like this ... riding the bus, eating at "ethnic" restaurants, and reading about "other cultures" or whatever ... I'm always an outsider.

But ... then again ... I feel like an "outsider" around my own friends half the time ... I feel outside of the elements of culture that are supposed to define me ... and for that matter ... I'm an outsider in my own body often enough, too ...

I guess I'm an "insider" when I turn my ever-jabbering thoughts off, and let myself just DO stuff, without THINKING so goddamn much.

I have to remind

myself to

live in the moment.

Oh, well ... at least I truly appreciate whatever teensy bits of "different ethnicities" that I am exposed to ... Hmmm ... what's this?

At least there are a couple places where I feel a sense of belonging.

END

HEAP

Basil Wolverton:
Producer of Preposterous Pictures of Peculiar People

Mark Frauenfelder

Art became an important part of my life when I saw my friend's mom rip a garishly colored sticker of a slack-jawed cartoon monster off his elementary school notebook. Wow! I knew had to get some of these rubbery, bloodshot-eyed, hyena-esque freak stickers for myself. In school, teachers confiscated the trading cards on sight, hating them even more than the ubiquitous *Wacky Packages* stickers. The cards were magic. We loved them, but even more importantly, *grown-ups hated them*!

It wasn't until the '70s, when I got my hands on *Plop!* magazine, that I learned the artist's name: Basil Wolverton.

ELBOWROOM CREATOR
When the subject is violently shoved, his blood pressure goes up, forcing brain cells up into the noggin knob, which action throws the switch of an enclosed battery-driven motor. Twin fans on the motor shaft blow highly-concentrated garlic fumes out thru the vents, suddenly resulting in a copious amount of room for the customer.

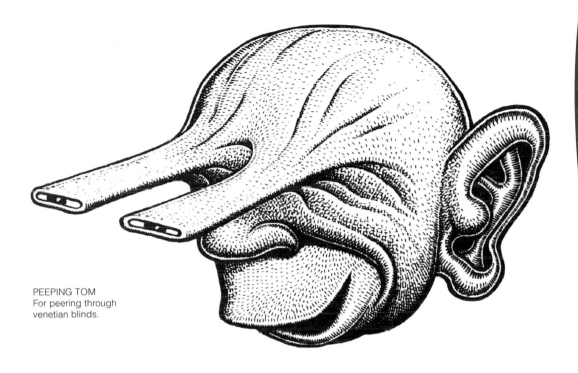

PEEPING TOM
For peering through
venetian blinds.

Born in Oregon in 1909, Basil lived in the Pacific Northwest his entire life. He wanted to be a vaudeville entertainer, and played ukulele and tap-danced for a while. Later, he became a newspaper reporter, and then produced a serious sci-fi comic called *Spacehawk*, which ran from the late '30s to mid '50s.

But nationwide notoriety really kicked in for Basil after he submitted a drawing of Lena the Hyena (a character from *Li'l Abner*) for a contest in *Life* magazine. Basil's entry was selected by a panel of judges that included Frank Sinatra, Boris Karloff, and Salvador Dalí. After winning the prize, he got tons of assignments from magazine, greeting card, and trading card publishers, all asking for the most hideous and goofy stuff he could dream up.

And he knew how to deliver the goods. To Basil, the human body was a pliable lump of clay that could be molded and twisted to adapt to any environmental insult heaped on it. Extra limbs, eyes, and heads were common on a Wolverton human. Techno-implants and appendages such as fans, sirens, water tanks, faucets, and jetpacks grew right out of people's skin. His characters always wore ecstatic expressions on their faces, as if they were pleased as all get out to have a hydraulic pump emerging from their stomachs.

Fans across the world shed a tear when the king of oddball art died in 1978. But, fortunately, many of today's best cartoonists learned their trade by copying Basil's art as children, and the gonzo spirit of this incredible artist lives on. A great collection of Basil's work can be found in the book *Wolvertoons*, edited by Dick Voll, and published by Fantagraphics. The price is $19.95. ◆

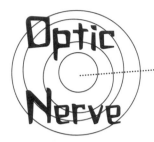

Optic Nerve

David Pescovitz

"Every story I do has some basis in real existence," says Adrian Tomine, a 21-year-old UC Berkeley English major and self-taught artist. His comic book, *Optic Nerve*, contains short stories of raw, realistic, and sometimes humorous ironic insights into life experiences: failed relationships, self-consciousness, fear, and neuroses. One story tells the tale of a couple's anniversary from the perspective of the

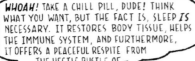

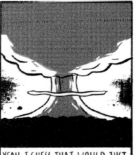

woman, who does not share her boyfriend's joy. Another focuses on a man whose borrowed leather biker jacket is his sole ticket to self-confidence.

"This may sound dopey and new agey, but my comics contain revelations," he says, laughing at his own word choice. "Putting the stories in a fictional veil, or seeing them from someone else's point of view, can clarify things for me."

Since high school, Tomine has spent a lot of time learning about himself. He found it difficult to relate to many of his peers at the "suburban high school for rich kids" he attended in Sacramento. Tomine says he "became an

introvert not by choice but by circumstance."

Uninterested in mainstream comic books, Tomine ordered self-published comics by mail. Underground artists like Terry Laban and Julie Doucet inspired him to begin filling up large sketchbooks with "rough ideas to learn how to express things through visuals."

Soon, he, too, began publishing his own comic book, *Optic Nerve*. As with most self-publishers, he released each issue of *Optic Nerve* on a shoestring budget and struggled to recoup the costs in $2 increments, the comic's cover price. In 1994, Canadian comic publisher Drawn and Quarterly began publishing *Optic Nerve*. Tomine

RECENTLY, I THOUGHT I'D STRUCK UPON THE PERFECT SOLUTION... I WOULD SLOWLY *WEAN* MYSELF OFF OF SLEEP, SETTING MY ALARM 10 MINUTES EARLIER EACH DAY.

BRILLIANT! THE CHANGE WILL BE SO GRADUAL, MY BODY WON'T EVEN NOTICE!

BUT ALAS, MY EXPERIMENT WAS A FAILURE: WITHIN TWO WEEKS, I WAS SICK AND EXHAUSTED!

I'VE DONE THE RESEARCH... I'VE EXPERIMENTED... I DON'T KNOW WHAT ELSE TO DO!

RIGHT HERE, BUDDY! Y'KNOW WHAT THIS IS, DUDE? IT'S *SPEED*, Y'DIG? A FEW LINES OF THIS SHIT AND YOU'LL BE UP FOR *DAYS*, BRO'!

DON'T YOU UNDERSTAND? I'M LOOKING FOR A *CURE*...NOT JUST TEMPORARY RELIEF! AS SOON AS THAT WORE OFF, I'D GO STRAIGHT TO SLEEP! FURTHERMORE, WHAT YOU'RE OFFERING ME IS AN ADDICTIVE, PARANOIA-INDUCING *DRUG*... HARDLY A SOLUTION TO THE QUANDARY AT HAND!

GO BACK TO L.A., YOU FUCKIN' *DRUGGIE!*

SO, UNTIL SOMEONE MAKES SOME *BREAK-THROUGH*, I'LL HAVE TO RESIGN MYSELF TO THE FACT THAT WITHOUT 7 HOURS OF SLEEP AND AT LEAST 3 CUPS OF COFFEE PER DAY, I'M WORTHLESS!

SIGH

IN FACT, ALL THIS TALKING HAS REALLY TIRED ME OUT!

I'M...HELPLESS...

WHAT A CURSE!

Z z z

GOOD-NIGHT!

Enjoy

hopes that he might be able to soon support himself by cartooning, like his friend, Dan Clowes, creator of *Eightball*, one of the most successful underground comics. Clowes recently moved to Berkeley, and the two coincidentally became neighbors. Tomine is heartened by the fact that Clowes can support himself and afford an automobile while "sleeping until two and drawing the rest of the day."

"This deal with Drawn and Quarterly isn't going to make me a rich star," he stresses. "But I'll be able to spend my time drawing the comic and not calling up some store in Canada asking for the $12 they owe me." ♦

The Incurably Crazy Comics of

Jim Woodring

David Pescovitz

Seattle comic book artist Jim Woodring says he has only been truly depressed once in his life, and that it lasted only for a few days. But the strangeness of his life eventually began to frighten him. In the early '80s, Woodring consulted a Jungian psychologist to sort through the symbols in search of a repressed memory.

After his first session, the shrink looked over two early issues of his comic book *Jim* and refused Woodring as a patient. Another psychologist Woodring met at a party was angered by that story, but after seeing the comic books, told Woodring he

would not accept him as his patient either. Neither would divulge a reason.

"I took the unwillingness of therapists to deal with me as a sign that I just shouldn't get involved with them," Woodring says. "I decided to live with allowing the repressed memory to remain a mystery."

Perhaps that was in the best interest of Woodring's sanity. The childhood Jim does remember couldn't have been more surreal if it were fabricated. His father was an engineer, his mother a toxicologist in the Los Angeles County Coroner's office. Woodring often hallucinated as a young boy—a huge staring eyeball hovered above him and grotesque faces peered over his bed voicing hideous curses. The voices continue to this day. Before he was even five years old, Jim drew images that were so frightening that he buried them in a hole in the ground.

"My childhood dreams were simple, smooth, and burnished with a very safe *visual* quality," he says, "even though they were frequently very terrifying. And I don't see that childlike form of expression as being safe and friendly at all. I don't see childhood as safe and friendly."

In 1970, after he graduated high school, Woodring enrolled in a night course in art history. One evening, *after* the professor's slide show, Jim saw the most influential image of his life on the projection screen. The image projected from Jim's mind was a cartoonlike giant frog (which appears on the cover of *Jim* #1). Woodring shrieked and ran out of the room, bringing a dramatic end to his structured education.

After fleeing college, he moved up and down the West Coast contributing to *Car-toons* magazine. In the early 1980s, Fantagraphic's publisher Gary Groth took notice of Woodring's self-produced "autojournal" and

gave him his own comic book.

In recent years, Woodring's work has journeyed into a polished Technicolor forest, home to the grotesquely cute Frank and Manhog—the former excruciatingly naive but with a violent temper, the latter an evil coward. Together, Woodring says, they form a complete being.

Woodring says his story ideas come to him like an unscratchable itch. When the itching starts, Woodring anxiously strides into the gaping ravine near his home. He stays there until his itch has been mentally scratched.

"I can't really say what it is that tells me when I've got it and when I haven't," Woodring says. "I don't really write them consciously. But when the whole thing is done I can look at it and there's some sort of interior logic."

After Frank and Manhog's latest tale has been excised, Jim might take a stroll around the Seattle neighborhood he and his wife chose because of its tranquil setting, or perhaps draw comic strips with his 8-year-old son. Maybe he'll make time to work on one of his intricate motorized

sculptures—like the wax replica of a foot with a protruding metal rod that rubs against a grinding wheel, the whole thing floating in a box of unpopped corn.

But inevitably, Jim Woodring will grow tired and retire to bed. Then the dreams will return . . . ◆

Jim Woodring:
5736 17th Avenue NE,
Seattle, WA 98105.

Fantagraphics Books:
7563 Lake City Way NE,
Seattle, WA 98115.

 *Notes*

"We hold these truths to be self-evident; that all men are created equal; that they are endowed with certain unalienable rights; that among these are life, liberty, and the pursuit of happiness . . . "

—Thomas Jefferson,
Declaration of Independence

ACKNOWLEDGMENTS

Pam Bricker
Julie Fishman
Kevin Kelly
Molly Ker
Jon Lebkowsky
Shalini Malhotra
Taha McVeigh
Paco Xander Nathan
Karen Nazor
Ward Parkway
Alan Rapp
Marny Requa
Douglas Rushkoff
Catherin Sawall
Mary South
Aoibheann Sweeny
Jessica Wing
    and . . .
Our families

CONTRIBUTORS

It is against the policy of the Schwa Corporation to release information. Please refer any questions you may have to our legal department. cc:bb (**Bill Barker**)

Colin Berry (cpberry@aol.com) lives in San Francisco, where he recently postered two-term California governor Pete Wilson. His clothes still smell like wheat paste.

Sarah Borruso (monkeybird@aol.com) is a San Franciscan with a paradoxical sense of humor.

Sean Carton (elrod@clark.net) is a writer, graphics weenie, and generally overeducated un-slack type. He wrote *The Virtual Worlds Quick Tour*, and thinks that his Macintosh is better than your goll-dern PC any day.

Jamie Chandler and **Robin Weiss** (415/929-0446) are photographers and designers who live in San Francisco. They work largely on free-lance projects and draw most of their inspiration from their dog, Jackson, who is also the CEO of their company, Dog Day Designs.

Dave Eggers and **Dave Moodie** (mightmag@aol.com), inventors of the intermittent windshield wiper, are currently sewing a quilt. They also do *Might* magazine.

Julie Fishman lives in San Francisco and is learning how to swim. She is currently working on her first book of short fiction.

Simson L. Garfinkel hacks English and Objective-C from his home in Central Square. For more information, check out http://pleasant.cambridge.ma.us

Early next year, **Danny Hellman** will be rocketed to the lunar surface to do battle with Wippy the two-headed death-slarg. He lives his life to save us all.

Andrew Hultkrans is a writer and self-admitted dilettante whose hemming and hawing about media, advertising, pop culture, and the occasional lunatic has appeared in *Artforum*, *Mondo 2000*, *IO* and *Fringeware Review*. He lives and slacks in San Francisco.

Marjorie Ingall was a member of the Shaun Cassidy Fan Club. Shut up.

Richard Kadrey (kadrey@well.com) writes and edits in his corner office at the fabulous GOMI BOY INDUSTRIES building. He has no qualifications for anything he does.

Stuart Mangrum is frequently mistaken for a member of the San Francisco Cacophony Society. His zine Twisted Times has been called *"The New Yorker* on powerful psychedelics." Reach him at stumangrum@aol.com

Paul Mavrides would do better if he only lived up to everyone else's expectations. Too bad for them. He awaits X-DAY with barely containable glee, his saucer ticket in hand.

Debra McClinton (415/552-4327), a San Francisco–based photographer, is determined to untangle her delicate web of wondering. Latest achievement? Discovered how many licks it takes to get to the middle.

Bart Nagel (barticus@well.com) is a freelance photographer and *Mondo 2000* art director, who lathers, rinses, and repeats before applying a two-minute conditioning treatment which volumizes and reconstructs.

Claudia Newell lives in NYC, combining foreign food packaging with psychological texts. Her spare time is spent practicing with her band, Dymaxion.

Kristy O'Rell (kristy@wired.com) has fond memories of high school and currently manages a geeky rock band appropriately called It Thing.

Ward Parkway: Born on a farm. Convinced we're all just four-dimensional protruberances of some sorta superdimensional hyperthang, but'll still play along with the simian notion of individuality.

David Pescovitz (pesco@well.com) lives in San Francisco and is an associate editor at *Blaster*. He also writes for *bOING bOING*, *Wired*, and *Zone*.

Jerod Pore (jerod23@well.com) programs mainframes in a trance state. When not getting paid, he reviews 100s of zines for *Factsheet Five* and still manages to publish *Poppin' Zits!*

Alan E. Rapp has written for *Wired*, *NewMedia*, and *I.D.* magazines, which doesn't deter him from writing overwrought fiction (still unpublished, of course). The films of Andrei Tarkovsky are his drugs of choice.

Chicago-area residents **Tom Roberts** and **Jim Siergey** (312/281-1388) have been writing and drawing their self-syndicated comic strip, *Cultural Jetlag*, since the '90s began.

Hal Robins is a cartoonist, illustrator, and broadcaster. He holds the enviable position of Master of Church Secrets in the Church of the SubGenius .

Robert Rossney (rbr@well.com) is a longtime computer weenie, online columnist for the *San Francisco Chronicle*, and co-author with his wife Sonia Simone of *Quiet Americans*.

Rudy Rucker (rucker@jupiter.SJSU.EDU) is a paradox: He appears never to be working, yet a wide range of things appear with his byline. His latest works: *The Hacker and the Ants* (SF novel) and *Artificial Life Lab* (book/software).

Isabel Samaras (izzycat@aol.com) paints dead presidents, debauched celebrities, and pornographic super-heroes. She has a line of "Devil Babe" ceramics called Rubber Claw.

In 1993, **Catherine Sawall** received her B.A. in anthropology and art history from Beloit College in Wisconsin. Because arctic temperatures are unhealthy for creative mutants, she migrated to California to become an intern for *bOING bOING*.

Michael Schwartz (meatyard@aol.com) is a free-lance photographer, raised in New Jersey and now living in San Francisco. If you hear screaming from a passing car, or see someone muttering to himself, it may very well be him.

Nathan Shedroff is the creative director at vivid studios in San Francisco and is coding information viruses in his spare time for widespread release.

John Shirley is the author of the *Eclipse Trilogy*. He spends a lot of time shuttling between Oakland and Los Angeles doing the Hollywood screenplay thing.

R. U. Sirius, co-founder of *Mondo 2000* and lead mutant insect for Mondo Vanilli (*IOU Babe*, Nothing Records) has co-authored *How to Mutate & Take Over the World* (Ballantine Books) and plays himself in the films *Virtual Love* and *Twists of the Wire*. He admires Christy Canyon, SubComandante Marcos, and Salvador Dalí.

Rev. Ivan Stang is one of the original co-sub-founders of the Church of the SubGenius. He preaches, when paid, nationwide. Interested SubGenii should investigate alt.slack on the Net.

Bruce Sterling (bruces@well.sf.ca.us) lives in Austin, Texas, and writes science fiction novels.

Betty Alexandra Toole, Ed.D., is the author of *Ada, the Enchantress of Numbers* (Strawberry Press). Her interests are creativity and technology. She has a consulting firm called Critical Connection in Sausalito, California.

Martini-drinking bachelor and boxing aficionado **Chip Wass** lives in Brooklyn, New York, where he tries in vain to stay out of trouble.

Jessica Wing (jessica@cyborganic.com) is the music editor of *bOING bOING*. She is also a writer, musician, dancer, prancer, and especially vixen.

Post-human artist **Shawn Wolfe** is proprietor of Beatkit Brands. His work has appeared in *Raygun*, *Urb*, *bOING bOING*, *Project X*, and on *HotWired*.

Jim Woodring is a self-educated cartoonist who mines his unconscious for the subject matter of his work. He writes and draws *Jim* for Fantagraphics Books.

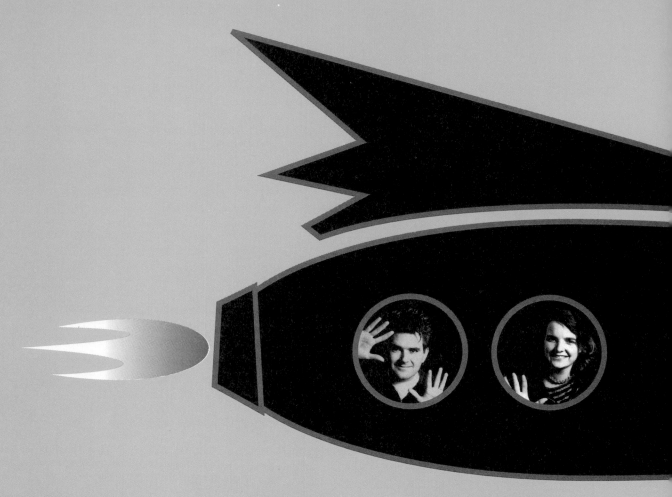

THE HAPPY MUTANTS

MARK FRAUENFELDER
(mark@well.com) is the co-founder of *bOING bOING* magazine and associate editor at *Wired*. His parents grounded him "for life" when he was 12 years old after he blew up the kitchen making smoke bombs.

GEORGIA RUCKER
(jorja@well.com) likes to do art on her machine. Scraps and peripherals stuff her room. Odds 'n' ends get scanned. She's now scrounging for new bytes in NYC.

Photos of Mark, Georgia, and Carla by Debra McClinton. Photo of Will by Marla Aufmuth. Illustration by Mark Frauenfelder.

WILL KRETH

(kreth@well.com), the first employee at *Wired* magazine, is now with *HotWired*, *Wired*'s station on the Internet. As a freelance writer his work has appeared in *Wired*, *Option*, *Arete*, and various places on the Net. He's building a Zimbabwean bass marimba to serenade the millennium.

GARETH BRANWYN

(gareth@well.com) is the senior ball-bouncer at *bOING bOING*. When he's not annoying the *bb* posse, he's locked away in his fortress of silicon co-authoring hypermedia (*Beyond Cyberpunk!*) and writing books (*Mosaic Quick Tour*, Ventana, 1994) and magazine pieces for *Wired*.

CARLA SINCLAIR

(carla@well.com) has been a *bOING bOING* kahuna since 1988. She's also tricked *Wired* into letting her be a frequent contributor for them. When she's off-duty, she's either lounging, luxuriating, or bullying the nearest nerd into playing Scrabble with her.

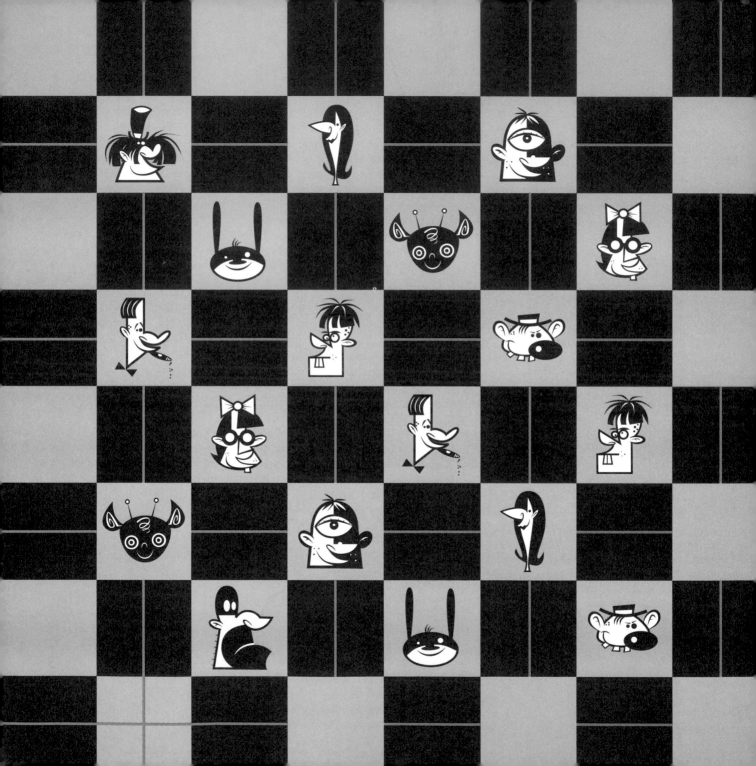